Relationship Skills

Woman's Missionary Union, SBC
Birmingham, Alabama

ROBERTA McBRIDE DAMON

Cover illustration by Cathy Robbins

Dewey Decimal Classification: 248.843

Subject Headings: CHRISTIAN LIFE–WOMEN
                  LEADERSHIP
                  HUMAN RELATIONS
                  WOMEN–PSYCHOLOGY

Series: Leadership Skills for Women

ISBN: 1-56309-082-1

W933105•0593•7.5M1

Church Study Course number 03352

Contents

A word to the reader

I have written this book for you. I hope you will like what you read and will find it useful. Through these pages, you will get to know me. I hope you will get to know yourself as well. You will find information here which will help you develop skills as you discover yourself and as you relate to others. I've included some exercises, so you need to read this with pen in hand. I also included some of my poetry, because sometimes that's the best way to speak the truth. Poetry inspires me, and I hope it will do the same for you. The subject is relationships. I hope you read, learn, and enjoy. Most of all, I hope that you will bless and be blessed through your relationships.

Roberta Damon
Richmond, Virginia, 1992

The Servant Song

We are travelers on a journey,
Fellow pilgrims on the road;
We are here to help each other
Walk the mile and bear the load.
I will hold the Christlight for you
In the nighttime of your fear;
I will hold my hand out to you,
Speak the peace you long to hear.

Sister, let me be your servant,
Let me be as Christ to you;
Pray that I may have the grace to
Let you be my servant, too.
Brother, let me be your servant,
Let me be as Christ to you;
Pray that I may have the grace to
Let you be my servant, too.

I will weep when you are weeping,
When you laugh I'll laugh with you;
I will share your joy and sorrow,
Till we've seen this journey thro'.
When we sing to God in heaven,
We will find such harmony,
Born of all we've known together
Of Christ's love and agony.
—Richard Gillard

Plea/Promise

I'm lonesome and I need a friend.
I feel like talking to someone.
I need to laugh a lot
And cry a little
With someone who won't think I'm crazy
Or irresponsible or stupid.
I need to talk to someone who'll meet me where I am
And accept me
Without judging or recrimination.
Right now I can't offer reciprocity.
This overwhelming need is suffocating me,
As you know, one who's drowning is not very giving.
Could you help me?
Would you?
I promise that tomorrow I'll be OK
And I'll do the same for you.

Who has never felt the need for a friend in a time of crisis or pain? How important is that bond with another person! Relationship is elemental.

We live out our lives within the context of relationships. Beginning with conception in our mother's womb, our very existence depends on the joining of two people who have chosen to be together. Our lives as infants and small children literally depend on the relationships we have with our primary caregivers. As we grow into children, the socialization process begins with playmates and schoolmates. We learn to tolerate. We learn to share. We learn that other people's needs are at least as important as our own. We might not like it, but we find it necessary to give up the infantile idea that the world revolves around us. We discover that we are not the center of the universe after all. What a shock to learn that there are other people to consider.

It was September 1958, in the model kindergarten at Southwestern Baptist Theological Seminary, where future children's workers did their practice teaching. Dr. Ann Bradford sat in a low chair in front of 40 wide-eyed five-year-old boys and girls. Crossed-legged on the huge oval braided rug, they participated in a dialogue with her.

"We have a problem," began Dr. Bradford. "We have so many boys and girls that even in our big room, we may be crowded. What do you think we ought to do?"

"We have to help each other," said Mimi.

"We could take turns," suggested Curt.

"We could work together," said Kristin.

Dr. Bradford smiled. "Those are good ideas. Do you know what the word *cooperate* means?" After a stimulating discussion of the word, Dr. Bradford asked, "Do you think we need some rules?"

The children suggested raising hands before speaking, saying *please* and *thank you*, and putting things away before coming to the big group.

"What if there is someone who just can't cooperate with us?" Dr. Bradford asked.

"We could put them in jail," suggested Bobby.

"We could send them home," said Becky.

"We could spank them," said David.

After much discussion, it was decided that anyone who just couldn't help would be asked to sit in a chair until ready to cooperate again.

I was a 23-year-old teacher-in-training that year. I was as wide-eyed as the children, observing Dr. Bradford's skill and wondering if I ever would be able to emulate her. Looking back on that endearing scene, I realize that it is a perfect picture of the reality of our lives: We are not alone. There are many of us. We need each other. We must learn to cooperate. There will always be those who will choose not to cooperate, and someone pays a price. This concept applies to a group of kindergarten children as well as the adult world.

Over a life span, relationships come to us in multiple sizes and shapes. Each one is like a swatch of fabric that makes up a crazy quilt—triangles, squares, and rectangles. The colors are vivid or muted. The patterns and textures represent an almost infinite variety—stripes, tweeds, plaids, checks, and solids. No two are alike. The threads that stitch them together are the events, experiences, attitudes, and memories which comprise our lives.

Some of our relationships will last forever. Some are of short duration.

In some, we invest our time and energy and love. In others, we maintain emotional distance. An acquaintance is different from a friendship, and a friend can be as close as a sister. The quality of the relationship depends on the depth of our investment.

The best relationships are dynamic. They change over time. Your relationship with your parents changed through your growing-up years. Your parents do not relate to you today as they did when you were a small child. Sometime during the young adult years, the contract between parents and their grown children is renegotiated. Marriages also change over the course of many years. The marital relationship changes from the honeymoon phase, through life's crises, to vintage mellowing. If we are wise, our relationships with our sisters and brothers evolve from childhood rivalry into adult caring and sharing. Friendships are formed and fade, or grow and endure.

The quality of relationships change as the patterns of our lives change. Relationships change by choice or through neglect. They change because we are not the same people at 50 that we were at 20. Relationships change as our needs change. Sometimes they change because something as simple as our address changes. Though we may be nostalgic about the good old days, we cannot go home again, and having left, our relationships may endure, but we are children no longer.

Relationship is the stuff of which life is made; we cannot separate ourselves from it. Our primary relationship is with God in whom we live, and move, and have our being. The Apostle Paul said that in God all things consist or hold together (Col. 1:17).

How skilled a pastry maker are you? I'm not good at it, but I know that simple ingredients are blended until they form the right consistency. I watched my mother a thousand times as she mixed the pastry dough with her hands. She knew by feel when it was right. She never missed; her pie crust was perfect every time. We have a pie crust relationship with God. All things hold together within that relationship and God never makes a mistake. With God, we have the only perfect relationship we'll ever experience on this earth—no thanks to us. It is God who is the same yesterday, today, and forever (Heb. 13:8)—gracious, dependable, loving, and forgiving.

Relationship is basic to our existence. Like kindergarten children, we learn day by day that we are valuable and that others have worth. We learn to get along with people not like ourselves. Our lives are made up of all the different people who touch us over the years and bring us memories—loving or painful. Each phase of our lives brings new associations. Some old friends move off center stage as new friends move on.

We are creatures of change. Sometimes we seek it; sometimes we avoid it. Sometimes it simply goes with the territory as a result of life decisions. Even as we deal with the trauma which change inevitably brings, we find our stability in a relationship with the unchanging God.

CHAPTER 1

Look around

A woman went into a bookstore to buy books for her grandchildren. She asked the clerk what would be suitable for a four-year-old and a five-year-old. The clerk responded with titles of several children's classics: *The Tales of Peter Rabbit, Winnie the Pooh,* some Dr. Seuss books.

"Those books are old," complained the customer.

"Yes," responded the clerk, "but the children are new."

If you have ever taken a walk with a very young child, you may have observed that the most mundane objects hold great fascination. The child is indeed new. To her, the world is new. As you read these pages, suspend your adult tendencies to critique and analyze. Be aware. Be curious. Be willing to learn. Be willing to play.

Words are fascinating. They allow us to conceptualize. Through language, we are able to define ourselves and are able to put our thoughts and concepts into meaningful form.

Word study-play

Re-la-tion-ship: the state of being related by kindred, affinity, or another alliance; the mutual exchange between two people or groups who have dealings with one another.

Think of at least six words that end in the suffix *ship*. List them below:

_____ship

_____ship

_____ship

_____ship

_____ship

_____ship

You may have thought of *fellowship, courtship, friendship, partnership, kinship, guardianship, dictatorship, governorship, authorship,* or *readership.* You may have thought of others. All have to do with relationship.

Even words like *craftsmanship* and *seamanship* have to do with a relationship to an activity.

The suffix *ship* means "ability" or "capability," so that *friendship* means "the ability to be or the capability of being a friend." *Courtship* means "the ability to court." *Worship* literally means "the ability to be of worth."

Relationship means "the ability to relate," to have mutual exchanges. It implies giving and receiving, initiative and respectful distance, mutuality and cooperation. Relationship has to do with one anothering.

One way we describe various relationships is by using the language of physiology. *Face-to-face* indicates interaction between two people. When we see two people face-to-face, we do not immediately know the nature of the interaction. If we say two people see "eye-to-eye," we mean that there is agreement in certain matters. If, however, we say two people are "eyeball-to-eyeball," our impression may be that there is confrontation. The Old Testament speaks of an "eye for an eye," and "a tooth for a tooth." This is the law of Lex Talions. Other phrases which describe confrontation or combat are *nose-to-nose*, *toe-to-toe*, *hand-to-hand*, or *head-to-head*. If we translate *head-to-head* into French, however, it becomes *tete-a-tete*. This gives an entirely different meaning to the relationship, "one of intimacy and closeness." *Tete-a-tete* is more akin to the English *cheek-to-cheek*, or *arm-in-arm*, which denotes romance. *Heart-to-heart* and *hand-in-hand* are terms which conjure up notions of love, talk, bonding, and friendship. *Mouth-to-mouth* is associated with life-saving resuscitation. *Neck-and-neck* denotes equality and competition. As you think about relationships, be aware of the nuances both in definitions and in the reality of the relationships themselves.

Characteristics of a healthy relationship

On a human level, there is no perfect relationship—no perfect friendship, no perfect marriage, no perfect working relationship. Good, solid, healthy relationships *do* exist. Three elements are present in a healthy relationship: mutuality, initiative, and respect.

Mutuality—A relationship cannot exist within one person. Relationship implies interchanges between or among people. Healthy relationships are mutual. Two people or groups of people either desire or are forced to relate one to another. Two women may choose to be in a friendship. Two other women may be co-workers who find that they are in daily contact and must work together. Although these two relationships are vastly different, the women will need to take a cooperative and mutual stance in order to accomplish their goals. Whether you find yourself in a friendship by choice, or in a working relationship by chance, mutuality and cooperation are necessary.

2

Initiative—Someone has to make the first move. If you are gregarious, you may find it easy to initiate conversations, plan activities, do most of the talking and maintenance work on a relationship. If you are more quiet and retiring, you may find yourself not wanting to intrude, being tentative about making suggestions, and waiting for the other person to initiate. You may be a loner who is drained by people. Since much of life requires interaction, we must all seek to meet each other halfway.

Respect—Keeping a respectful distance is a necessary ingredient for any healthy relationship. Being considerate of the other person's personal space is important. There are those who consistently invade the space of other people either by suffocating with too much warmth and nurturing or by coming across as bossy or demanding. The phrase *come across* is particularly apt. There is an invisible line in any relationship that marks the division between what is permissible and what is intolerable. We need to ask permission, wait to be invited, and otherwise be respectful of the rights of other people.

What we get from relationships

Why are relationships so important? What do we derive from relationships? What do relationships do for us?

From relationships, we get **stimulation**. From infancy, we need physical, intellectual, and emotional stimulation. Without being stimulated by our senses and by human contact, we would not develop into functioning people. Relationship provides stimulation to our senses and to our sense of well-being. Some people tolerate and need more stimulation in their relationships than others. Outgoing people thrive on movement and activity. Quiet, reserved people might prefer less contact with other people and may have a real need for time alone. City dwellers are often subjected to over stimulation—too much noise, too many people, too much pressure—causing distress. There is no right amount of stimulation within relationships, but most people become aware of the level they need or can tolerate.

From relationship, we get **affirmation**. Even the most confident person needs affirmation from others. Emotional support is provided when affirmation is given. We develop a sense of self when we see approval reflected in the eyes of someone who affirms us. This begins in infancy when mother and baby gaze into each other's eyes with utter approval. If we begin life this way, we begin to feel confident about our own value. As we develop our sense of self, we are able to offer emotional support and affirmation to others. A healthy cycle of affirmation begun in infancy can produce healthy adult relationship.

From relationship, we get **recognition**. Every child who has ever had a smiling face stamped on a test paper knows the joy of being recognized for a job well done. Positive relationships give us a similar sense of well being. If you choose to be in a relationship with me, I feel validated in my sense of worth. I am somebody. Theologically, this is what God does for us in Christ.

From relationship, we get **consultation**. When decisions need to be made, a "trusted other" can be counted on to listen, evaluate, and advise. Since no one has all the answers or expertise in every area, consulting with another person makes sense. Seeing a situation from another perspective gives new insight. Relationship becomes a resource for information, feedback, and clarification. Talking, listening, being heard and understood are benefits of being in relationships.

From relationship, we get **consolation**. When life brings pain and loss, family and friends gather to offer consolation and comfort. Emotional support in time of crisis is available through relationships. Anyone who has suffered the shock and grief associated with a death in the family understands what it means to be surrounded by a loving church family. Giving and receiving consolation happens within relationships.

Within relationship, we find **realization**. Perhaps you have heard someone say, "I find realization in my work," or "I find my greatest realization in my children." Realization is a sense of accomplishment and satisfaction—a job well done. Relationship provides a place to share that realization which gives it meaning.

In a relationship, we can engage in **conversation**. Listening and talking, understanding and being understood is life enhancing. Different points of view, different opinions, different outlooks, different experiences—these are designed to enrich our lives. Our relationships provide us with opportunities to love and learn.

Within a relationship, we find **communion**. The word *communion* literally means "joined together." We are joined together as we converse and when we are silent. We commune in various ways. In a relationship where we know and are known, a nod of the head, a wink, a smile, a simple gesture, will take on meaning for the recipient. We communicate information, feelings, and opinions in a never-ending flow. It is part of what makes us human. Relationship offers us communion with others. Joy is doubled and sorrow halved when we share it with a friend.

Proximity in relationships

Are you a people watcher? Do you enjoy observing people in public places? In our society there are unspoken, but clearly understood, distances people maintain in various settings.

Intimate space: Intense activities take place here. A whisper can be heard at this distance. Lovers cuddle and kiss at this distance. Friends hug and touch here. The sorrowing are comforted in this space. People in intimate space are touching or they are relating with very little literal space between them. Two people in intimate space are never more than a foot-and-a-half apart.

Interpersonal space: Less intimate conversations occur here between friends. Touch is more limited, and speech takes the form of a normal conversational tone. Distance between people here is between one-and-a-half and four feet.

Social space: More formal interchanges take place in this space. These are typical interactions between business associates, customers with service people, and strangers in conversation. The physical distance here is 4 to 12 feet.

Public space: When your pastor is preaching from the pulpit, his voice is geared to reach a congregation. While he may be warm and enthusiastic in his manner, the exchange between him and a worshiper in the pew is not a personal one. Teachers who lecture or politicians "on the stump" are all within the public space. When you call a greeting to a neighbor, you are within the public space. It is difficult to read facial expressions or to gauge a person's mood within this space. Public space means speaker and listener are more than 12 feet away from each other.

The setting dictates how we relate to another person. Cultural considerations including gender and nationality also come into play. If two North American women friends are conversing, they will sit or stand at a distance that is understood to be comfortable for both. They will look each other in the eyes, and it is permissible for one or the other of them to touch the arm of the person with whom they are talking. There will be approximately equal listening and talking. If the nationality is changed from North American to Northern European or British, the distance is automatically widened and there will be less touching. If the two women conversing are Latin American or Mediterranean, they will converse more animatedly and the distance between them narrows to inches.

If we take away either of the women and add a man, the whole equation changes. In every culture, when women and men are interacting, there are understood taboos concerning touching, distance, eye contact, and body posture. Contrary to popular opinion, in male/female interaction, men talk more than women do. Men are more likely to interrupt women than they are to interrupt men.

In public, if personal space is invaded by a stranger (on a crowded bus or airplane), observe the distancing tactics people employ to indicate an unwillingness to be engaged in conversation: a closed facial expression, sleep or feigned sleep, reading a book or newspaper, turning the body slightly away from the other person, staring into space, using earplugs or earphones. These are clear signals that a person is staking out personal space even in a crowd.

We begin to relate to another person by the simple act of looking. When the person looks back, eye contact is made and a relationship begins. It can begin in infancy between mother and baby—life's first love relationship. It can begin a different kind of love relationship in adolescence. It happens in a classroom when a teacher holds a student spellbound and fascinated. Dr. William David Kirkpatrick at Southwestern Baptist Theological Seminary, often said to a classroom full of students, "Put your pens down. Don't write. I want you to get this. Look at me." Eye contact can create understanding between teacher and student. It can begin a friendship or a courtship. It can enhance a kinship. A relationship begins when we "listen with our eyes."

How relationship happens

How does relationship happen? Sometimes, of course, a relationship just happens. You are related by blood or by marriage to another person and a relationship is inevitable. The quality of a relationship, however, is determined by **intentionality**. I may have a sister-in-law in a distant state. We may see each other five times in a lifetime. Do I have a relationship with her? Only superficially. An intentional relationship implies a mutual decision, either spoken or by tacit agreement. Two people decide to invest themselves to a degree in their dealings with each other.

There are levels of relationship, not determined by kinship. A blood sister may not have the same relationship with you that a best friend enjoys. Because you were born of the same parents does not automatically guarantee that you will relate well to each other. More likely, the experiences you shared as children and adolescents growing up in the same family will either bond you to, or estrange you from, one another.

Relationship may be anything from an acquaintance to a casual friendship, to a best friendship. We have acquaintances, friends, close friends, and best friends. Romantic relationships fall into another category altogether—although lovers can be friends.

Geography may determine how much contact you have with another person, but it is not the determining factor in the level of the relationship. Extremely deep and meaningful relationships often extend over time and distance. A heart-to-heart bond may be forged early, and in spite of the miles that separate two people, the relationship endures.

6

Frequency of contact has less to do with a relationship than intentionality. You may see a neighbor every day—wave, smile, call a greeting—but you do not have an intentional, in-depth relationship with that person. A healthy, intentional relationship implies mutual choice—an agreeing to relate.

My friends and acquaintances

List your closest friends. (Some people will say they have 235 best friends. This is impossible. No one has time and energy for that many close friends. List 1 to 5 persons you consider closest to you. These may include friend, blood relatives, and/or a spouse.)

1. _____
2. _____
3. _____
4. _____
5. _____

Freeze frame

Where would you place yourself in this frame? In relation to yourself, where would you place the five persons in your life with whom you have the most important relationships? Let circles represent you and those five other persons.

Who is central in the frame? Who is central in your life? Who is closest to you? Why? Who was your first friend?

Which childhood friend do you remember fondly?

List people who were good friends years ago, but with whom you do not presently maintain close contact.

1. _____
2. _____
3. _____
4. _____
5. _____

List other good friends (5 to 15 persons).

1. _____
2. _____
3. _____
4. _____
5. _____
6. _____
7. _____
8. _____
9. _____
10. _____

List your social network. (This will include 15 to 30 persons including aunts, uncles, cousins, co-workers, church friends, etc.)

_____
_____
_____
_____
_____
_____
_____

You can probably name 100 to 1,000 acquaintances.
You can probably think of five to ten familiar strangers (the mailman, the man at the supermarket, etc.).

1. _____
2. _____
3. _____
4. _____
5. _____

In the center of the wheel on the next page, write your first name or your nickname. In each of the designated sections, write one name of a person in your life from each category. Under their names, write a gift which each person brings into your life. (It might read something like this: sister—Carolyn—love; best friend—Susie—joy; good friend—Janet—laughter; friend—Mark—good advice; acquaintance—Mrs.

Johnson—a smile; co-worker— Sandra—understanding; neighbor—Mr. Sanders—security; familiar stranger—mailman— consistency; relative—Aunt Mable—continuity.)

Pause to give thanks for people in your life (in memory, presently, forever) who bring gifts to you. Remember. Feel the joy. Choose one person. Write and send a note of thanks for her contribution to your life.

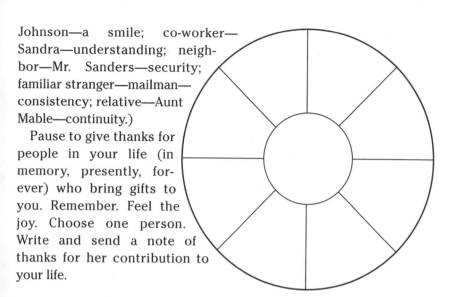

The way women relate

Women are seen as naturally good at relationships. It is often the woman who does the major portion of the maintenance work on a marriage. Most often she is the one who says to her spouse, "We need to talk." In female same-sex friendships, women tend to talk about personal, intimate matters. With a trustworthy woman friend, they engage in self-disclosure. It is not so much what we have in common that bonds us with another, but rather the ability to self-disclose. Female friendships are characterized by mutual understanding and a willingness to be there for the other person.

In the past 20 or 30 years, the study of gender difference has emerged as an area of psychological study. Debate rages over why men and women are the way they are and how they got that way. Are women genetically programmed to be what is considered feminine, or are they socialized in ways that produce characteristic results? No one has found a definitive answer, but some interesting observations have been made.

From infancy, female infants gaze into the eyes of their mothers more than do male infants. Girls look each other in the eyes when they converse, while boys tend to look away from each other avoiding eye contact. In contrast to adult male interactions with other males, adult female friendships thrive on eye-to-eye contact. The same is true of male/female interactions in courtship.

Children of elementary school age are rule-oriented and have a highly developed sense of fair play. Boys will argue over the rules of the game and negotiate a settlement. Girls defer more to each other and will suspend play rather than argue about the rules. As adults, women typically take a cooperative stance while working together on projects, however, they have been acculturated to compete with each other for male attention. Men tend to compete with each other in every area and are often heavily invested in winning.

Females of all ages are more verbal than males. They tend to talk on a more personal level than do males, beginning at adolescence and continuing through adulthood.

Male friendships tend to center around activities or sports, whereas female friendships are more likely to be based on intimate verbal exchange. Women are much more likely to report having a same-sex best friend than are males.

Women over 50 tend to identify themselves within their relationships. If asked, "Who are you?" they are most likely to say something like, "I am Mary Johnson, Paul Johnson's wife." Younger women are more likely to identify themselves as men have traditionally done—by what they do vocationally: "I'm Mary Johnson. I am a computer analyst for Duckworth International." These differences do not mean better than or worse than. It simply means that men and women take a different view of life, and their relationships are affected by those views.

List six words that are descriptive of women in general.

1. _____
2. _____
3. _____
4. _____
5. _____
6. _____

List six words that are descriptive of men in general.

1. _____
2. _____
3. _____
4. _____
5. _____
6. _____

If you look carefully, you will discover that you have written words not exclusively descriptive of one sex or the other. What you have written about men and women are descriptive of some women and some men. You have written a list of human characteristics. We can conclude, then, that women can be all of the above.

Stereotypically, women have been negatively characterized as dependent, overly emotional, weak, flirtatious, talkative, shallow, and jealous.

Men have been labeled, often unfairly, as cold, distant, unemotional, aggressive, controlling, and ruthless. Both women and men can be all or any of these things.

Therefore, women can be:	or women can be:
selfless yet assertive	assertive yet selfless
meek yet strong	strong yet meek
modest yet confident	confident yet modest
calm yet effective	effective yet calm
kind yet firm	firm yet kind
flexible yet responsible	responsible yet flexible
givers yet receivers	receivers yet givers
listeners yet talkers	talkers yet listeners
learners yet teachers	teachers yet learners

Women's talk and women's work

We are "labourers together with God," Paul reminds us in 1 Corinthians 3:9. While the Bible teaches that the laborer is worthy of his (her) hire, women's work has been consistently undervalued. Her value in the marketplace is less than her male counterpart's. Her salary is consistently lower than a man's even though they do the same work. Her college degree will earn her approximately what a man's high school diploma will earn him. Many women will find themselves in pink collar jobs—nursing, secretarial work, school teaching, etc. When a profession becomes feminized, salaries decrease. Conversely, when men take over jobs traditionally held by women, salaries and titles are upgraded.

Just as women's work has been denigrated, women's conversation has been trivialized as "girl talk." It is seen as idle chatter, shallow talk, having little or no substance. We need to begin to see women's talk for what it is—the glue that holds relationships together, a mutual sharing of deeply-felt emotions, important speaking-into-being the realities of our lives. Finding a voice means finding an identity. Finding an identity means valuing ourselves, the language that we speak, and the work that we do. We need to expect others to recognize our worth.

Say the word *labor* in a group of women and see what immediately comes to mind. Birthing is what women were created to do. Their birthing, however, is not limited to children. Birthing creative ideas and concepts, organizations, and movements, is also within the domain of women. Most often the birthing process is a cooperative effort. For centuries it was the female midwife who helped in the delivery of babies. Women have discovered, or perhaps they have always known, that whether birthing babies or ideas, the way women work most effectively is together, in a spirit of cooperation—within relationships.

CHAPTER 2

Look in/Look across

There is nothing more important than having an identity separate from others. Know yourself is an age-old admonition. Women have often been lost in the shuffle of conflicting demands. They tend to become the person-of-the-moment based on immediate needs—counselor, listener, cook, laundress, secretary, errand runner, lover, problem solver. It is acceptable for bosses, husbands, children, teachers, colleagues, friends, and all others to have needs, but women often feel that it is not acceptable for them to have needs which limit others' access. Many women deny their own needs in order to be of service to everybody and anybody else. There is no boundary setting.

A woman may ask, "Where do I begin and where do others end?" This is exactly where all newborns begin life: What is I and not I? When a woman begins to question and to define herself, she is leaving the passive infantile state, and becoming her own person. She is defining her own identity. Looking inward is a prerequisite for feeling comfortable inside one's own skin.

My profile
Fill in the blanks with the first thought that comes to mind.

1. When I was a child I always wanted to _____
_____

2. My father and I _____
_____

3. My mother and I _____
_____

4. One thing I remember is _____
_____

5. If I could do anything I wanted I would _____
_____

6. One thing that makes me laugh is _____

7. I get angry when _____

8. I am impatient with _____

9. Religion in my life is _____

10. I love _____

11. The thing I most fear is _____

12. I have fun when _____

13. Intimacy is _____

14. The most embarrassing thing that ever happened to me was _____

15. I hate _____

16. I believe _____

17. Something that is important to me is_____

18. I laugh when _____

19. I have the ability to _____

20. One thing I like about me is _____

21. One thing about me I would like to change is _____

22. God is _____

23. My church is _____

24. For me to forgive is _____

25. I am the kind of person who _____

Look back over your answers. Identify points of pain. Find areas of joy. What do your answers indicate about your self-esteem? What do they tell you about the kind of person you are?

During our lives, we develop from infants to toddlers to children to adolescents to adults. There is an obvious progression. It is easy to observe the physical changes that take place in people as they progress from stage to stage. Less obvious are the emotional, spiritual, and psychological stages. In each stage of human development, there are tasks which need to be accomplished. A healthy and functioning person will have good self-knowledge and a fairly accurate view of how she comes across to others. She will have a sense of her own identity and know how to affirm herself and accept affirmation from others.

How do you identify yourself? How do you define yourself? What are your likes and dislikes? To check out your self-knowledge, underline the words and phrases which apply to you.

I like:

parties

staring at the ocean

praying wherever I am

many different kinds of people

I feel most comfortable with:

a planned prayertime

people I know well

arriving at appointments early

giving to others

setting and meeting goals for myself

seeking advice before I act

I prefer:

to play things by ear

quiet

meeting new people

organizing an event

doing things myself (being independent)

chairing the committee

I don't like:

unplanned events

a full calendar

a roomful of strangers

to be called on without warning

I find it difficult to tolerate:

someone resting while I'm working

someone working while I'm resting

a messy room

people who won't ask for directions when they are lost

people who squeeze the toothpaste tube in the middle

I react positively to:

punctuality

a relaxed atmosphere

an orderly room

wearing jeans and going barefoot

people who are properly groomed

I have the ability to:

understand how others feel

balance my checkbook

read and fold a map

ask for directions if I'm lost

read people

confront others with their unacceptable behavior

"just know" something without being told

analyze a situation and solve problems

It is difficult for me to:

lose weight

plan ahead

talk to people

be center stage

tolerate laziness

Taken together, the words and phrases you chose give a profile of your values and your preferences. Go back and read aloud in paragraph form. After each statement, think of a positive word that describes the descriptive phrase. It may read something like this: "I like parties and many different kinds of people (gregarious). I feel most comfortable with arriving at appointments early (punctual) and giving to others (sensitive/kind). I prefer organizing an event, doing things myself, and chairing committees (competent). I don't like unplanned events or to be called on without warning (structured). I find it difficult to tolerate someone resting while I'm working (industrious/fair minded). I also can't tolerate a messy room (orderly). I react positively to punctuality, an orderly room, and people who are properly groomed (organized). I have the ability to balance my checkbook and analyze and solve problems (intelligent/capable). It is difficult for me to tolerate laziness (hardworking).

Circle the symbol on the next page which best describes you. Write in the space beneath the symbol three reasons you chose that one.

1. _____
2. _____
3. _____

If you chose the **square**, this might suggest that you are a person who is comfortable with structure and boundaries. These folk often are good at organizing and planning. They probably need to know what the policy is and which procedure is most acceptable. "Square" people are good at logistics. They are dependable and know how to get things done. They are often good at details and have acquired much useful knowledge. They know how to do things and are skillful at administration. They are solid and dependable.

The **circle** is the universal symbol of completion. It has no beginning and no end. It is a symbol of the eternal. "Circle" people are often inclusive. They have a spiritual nature and often are meditative. While they are good at setting boundaries in relationships, they may not need or want rules. "Circle" people are intuitive and insightful.

The **infinity symbol** is a circle turned on its side and slightly twisted. It suggests eternity. There is no beginning and no ending to this symbol. It suggests flow. Applied to relationship, it gives a perfect picture of mutuality and reciprocity. It is a symbol of the seasons of the year which flow one into another in a never-ending cycle. It is a symbol of acceptance, release, openness. "Infinity" people often put a high value on relating well to others. They are accepting and want to be understood and accepted.

The **squiggle** suggests a free spirit. The direction is forward. "Squiggle" people are movers. They are often cheerleaders for others. They put humor at the top of the list of things that are important. They live a somewhat unconventional life-style, or they often wish that they could. They are seen as flighty by some more serious-minded people, but they will bring laughter and joy to an otherwise dull situation.

Answer the following questions with a word or phrase:
1. What do you fear?

_____

_____

The ultimate fear for human beings is the fear of death. We are the only creatures who are equipped to understand that we will not live in these bodies forever, we will all face physical death. One of the miracles of being human is to know this, the hope of heaven notwithstanding, and to still function—to go about our daily lives without going insane.

Babies have a primitive fear which is built in for their own protection. Even though they have no language, babies instinctively know that if mother, or some other caretaker, does not provide food and care, they will die. The primitive brain is programmed to fear neglect unto death. If needs are not met, the baby cries. Infants have no mechanism to distinguish between life-threatening neglect and mother's unavoidable five-minute delay.

Like infants, adults feel fear when they feel their basic, legitimate needs are ignored. Even though an adult knows with her more highly developed brain that she will not die, the most primitive portion of the human brain does not have a sense of time. It does not know the person is now grown up. It simply triggers danger, and the most primitive response is, "I'll die." On rare occasions, of course, one's life may be in danger, but more often it is not. Life-threatening is a gun to the head, or an incurable disease, not day-to-day situations within relationships.

Put your fear into perspective. We say, "If I can't have him, I'll die," or "I can't live without her." That is not literally true. If my mother does not love me, I will not die. I may be deeply wounded. I may wish that it could be otherwise, but I will not die. I may be in such emotional pain that I think death would be preferable to the pain I am suffering, but I will not die. When you are afraid, ask yourself, "Will I die from this?" It is amazing the comfort and courage you will derive from knowing that, with God's help, you will survive whatever is facing you.

People are paralyzed by fears—fear of failure, fear of not being good enough, fear of loss, fear of abandonment, fear of death, fear to the point of phobia. Fear prevents normal, healthy functioning. The message of the gospel is the antithesis of fear. "Do not be afraid," said the angel to the shepherds, "for behold, I bring you good tidings of great joy" (Luke 2:10). "Do not be afraid," said Jesus walking on the water toward his frightened disciples, "It is I" (Mark 6:50). "My peace I give to you" (John 14:27). What do you fear?

2. What makes you angry?

What is your anger style? Do you have a short fuse or a long one? Do you tend to explode or simmer? Do you take your anger out on someone not directly responsible for it? If you have carried lifelong anger toward a parent, you may take it out on a husband, a child, or a co-worker. Are you aware of long-term anger you carry? Are you an irritable person who wakes up spoiling for a fight? Are you mad at the world?

Biologically, anger is nothing more than energy. It is an emotion which people find inconvenient at best and devastating at worst.

The anger curve is a graphic representation of what happens to you when you become angry. It looks like this.

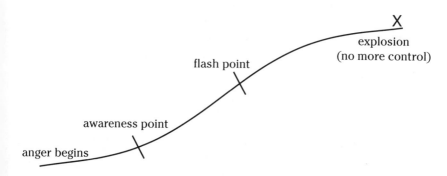

If your anger begins at the far left of the curve, gauge the time/circumstances between that point and the point at which you become aware of it. Anger may have been simmering for years. From the awareness point to the flash point five seconds or five years may pass. The flash point is the point beyond which there is no more control. The curve serves to help you decide how you can be aware sooner. The earlier you are aware of your feelings, the more control you can assume over them. This is not an exercise to help you stop being angry. It is to help you decide a healthy way to handle your anger.

The question is, Do my emotions control me and dictate my behavior, or do I control my emotions? We cannot help the way we feel; our feelings are valid. We can begin to control the way we think. We can control our behavior. We do have choices. What makes you angry?

3. How do you express affection?

Some people are comfortable expressing affection by their actions. Doing kind things is a legitimate way of saying, "I care about you." These are often overlooked or not interpreted as expressions of affection. If you grew up in a family of huggers and touchers, you are probably comfortable with physical expressions of affection. If as a child you were told, "I love you," or "you are the sweetest little thing," you probably

19

express affection to others verbally. If your family of origin was reserved about expressing affection, you may be uncomfortable with a verbal or physical expression of love. Verbal "I love yous" may sound insincere to you. Physical affection may make you uneasy. Unfortunately, in our society, the expression of affection has become sexualized. Television and movies deal with adult themes. Advertising leans heavily on sexuality in order to sell products. Our children grow up bombarded with sexually charged messages. People tend to be wary of any expression of affection for fear of being misunderstood or sued.

Against this cultural background, gender differences play an important role in our attitudes toward the expression of affection. Within the marriage relationship, men tend not to separate sexual expression from love, while women tend to believe love and sex are quite different. Women believe that a sexual expression is one of many ways of showing love for their husbands. Obviously, expressing affection for a husband, a friend, a child, or a parent, will differ. One of the marks of a healthy, functioning family is the ability to distinguish among these differences. How do you express affection?

4. What wounds you?

_____

_____

Read the following poem. Do you identify with it?

Pain

There are words—
Words, perhaps, that should be said in all truth and in all honesty,
That cut so deeply into the essence of the soul
It is as if flesh is sliced by jagged glass,
As if viscera sustains a wound from which pours life
The wound is left open and unattended.
There are acts—
Perhaps righteous—who can say?
That strike the senses with such force
The body trembles,
The eyes fill and spill,
The mouth goes dry,
The throat constricts,
The stomach knots.
It is as if the psyche,
Having no tangible place to feel the pain
Translates through every nerve-end,
Agony of soul into physical anguish.
It is as if one stands in sun's benevolent warmth,
Yet feels such cold that nothing can allay the chill.
Words and acts—sometimes necessary, no doubt,
Said or perpetrated in the best interest of all concerned,
Are nevertheless, like a hard, undeserved slap across the mouth,
So that in stunned disbelief,
The eyes widen at the shock,
In bewilderment and heartsickness
One awaits the inevitable discoloration and swelling.
Well, bruises and swelling subside.
The heart is a muscle—it can't really break.
Grief passes.
Hurt can be endured.
One lives on—scarred, marked, wiser perhaps—
More wary and less eager to open oneself to pain;
But one lives.

Wounding is a part of the human condition. Some people are so well defended against pain that they literally cannot feel it. We are wounded by harsh words, hateful looks, or cold silence, if not by rape, incest, or battering. We are also wounded by caustic humor, sarcasm, or ridicule.

Females in our society have been granted the right to weep, but weeping is seen almost universally as a sign of weakness. What makes you weep? What wounds you?

5. What makes you laugh?

The benefit of humor in our lives is well documented. It is an area over which we have some measure of control. We choose our humor style: slapstick, puns, jokes, quirky twists of phrases, etc. Look through the comics section of your Sunday newspaper. Which of the comic strips do you enjoy most? Political humor is a kind of social commentary depicted in several syndicated strips. Family situations lend themselves to humorous treatment. The human condition is embodied in both of these. Choosing your preferred comic strip is an indication of your taste and personality style.

Laughter has been called "the saving grace," "internal jogging," and "the best medicine." It is true that when we laugh, our bodies release endorphins into the blood stream which have a measurable positive effect on our health. It also serves as the lubricant that enhances our relationships. We sometimes lament that our society is entertainment and fun oriented, but it is not all bad. Laughter helps us endure the pain of life. Healthy humor helps us maintain a positive outlook on life. We use humor to entertain ourselves and others, to reduce tension, to express warmth, to put others at ease, to facilitate conversation, to lessen anxiety, and to help cope with difficult situations. It is an integral expression of our joy. We miss the point if we miss the laughter. What makes you laugh?

6. What is important to you?

What are your priorities? What do you value? The answers to these questions give insight into your personality. Moral, ethical, and religious considerations come into play in this question. On a less basic plane, personal tastes and preferences need to be considered. What is important to you?

Your answers to the previous six questions provide a fairly accurate picture of who you are and in which directions you need to grow.

Being assertive

One area many women need to explore is their level of assertiveness. Assertiveness has been confused with aggression. Aggression is fueled by anger and the need to control others. Assertiveness is healthy self-confidence—realizing you have strength and acting on that knowledge. Mark each statement true or false.

☐ True ☐ False   1. I hesitate to call a friend for fear she may not want to talk to me.

☐ True ☐ False   2. When I have a strong opinion about a subject, I do not hesitate to express myself.

☐ True ☐ False   3. I think of myself as lacking in self-confidence.

☐ True ☐ False   4. If someone does not do a good job, they should be fired and replaced.

☐ True ☐ False   5. I sometimes feel I am not worthy of affirmation from others.

☐ True ☐ False   6. I discipline myself.

☐ True ☐ False   7. I do not like the way I look.

☐ True ☐ False   8. I believe everyone should follow the same rules.

☐ True ☐ False   9. I sometimes feel I have nothing to say that is worth hearing.

☐ True ☐ False   10. I see myself as more often right than wrong.

☐ True ☐ False   11. I sometimes think of myself as stupid.

☐ True ☐ False   12. People should either do their work or get out of the way and let someone else do it.

☐ True ☐ False   13. I believe other people have more to contribute than I do.

☐ True ☐ False   14. I get angry when I have to wait in line.

☐ True ☐ False   15. I am often depressed.

☐ True ☐ False   16. I am often irritable.

☐ True ☐ False   17. I do not want to intrude on others.

☐ True ☐ False   18. I consider myself a person of high energy.

☐ True ☐ False   19. I am often tired.

☐ True ☐ False   20. I believe in "telling it like it is."

Scoring: Count the number of even numbered questions you marked true and write the number in the box at the left. Count the number of odd numbered questions you marked true and write that number in the box on the right.

Even numbered ☐   Odd numbered ☐

If you answered true to seven or more odd numbered statements, you probably need to change the way you think and talk about yourself. Begin to believe you are a worthy and valuable person, created and redeemed by God. Claim the blessings God has for you and confidently become more assertive in your relationships. This does not mean you become abrasive, but that you develop a new style of relating to others which encourages your growth as a fully functioning human being.

If you answered true to seven or more of the even numbered statements, you probably tend to come across as overly aggressive. Hesitate before you speak, and ask yourself if what you have to say is respectful and kind. Read Galatians 5:22-23 and check the fruits of the Spirit (love, joy, peace, patience, gentleness, goodness, faith, meekness, self-control) against your behavior.

Seeing yourself as others see you

Read the following paragraph through once. Then do the exercise. It does not matter if you do not remember every question.

Sit in a quiet, comfortable place. Breathe deeply. Close your eyes. Picture yourself in the most recent face-to-face conversation you had with a friend. Picture your friend. What is she wearing? What are some of her mannerisms? What expressions do you read in her face? How does she use her voice to convey different emotions? What words would you use to describe her? Trade places with your friend. Put yourself in her place. Become your friend as she interacts with you. See yourself from her perspective. How would she describe you? What words come to mind? Would she say that you are bright, interested, quiet, angry, cooperative, combative? How do you think you come across to her? Take three deep breaths. Open your eyes. How were you feeling during that encounter? Who was comfortable? Who was in pain or feeling angry? Who was left out or ignored? Who was understood and valued? Who was put down?

Trying to see ourselves as others see us is important to our functioning within relationships. Understanding our own feelings also helps us to process why we act the way we act. We have choices. We can learn to make good ones. Self-knowledge means knowing what you like, what you are comfortable with, what you are good at (including your spiritual gifts), and how you prefer to do things. It invariably affects the way you relate to other people. You need to be able to name your own strengths. You also need to recognize those areas in your life that you would like to change. If you know yourself well, you have an idea of how others see you. You also have some idea of how you would like for others to see you. You can begin to be comfortable walking around in your own skin. You can accept yourself as a growing, changing person. You can accept yourself as valued by God and worthy of acceptance by others.

Differences in personal style

What a dull world this would be if everyone were alike. There is infinite variety in the human family. One difference lies in the area of personal style—the ways people operate within their relationships.

Examine the following contrasts:

Some people perceive life in polarities: black/white, right/wrong, good/bad, win/lose. Others find all kinds of leeway, extenuating circumstances, and grey areas.

Some need time alone to recoup their energies, to meditate, to rest, to be quiet. Others can't tolerate solitude. They seek out excitement. They want to be where the action is and they are energized by people in crowds, music, and laughter.

Some are precise, analytical, and methodical. Others are relaxed, unhurried, and comfortable.

Some are rule and policy oriented. Others dislike rules and prefer to "play it by ear."

Some are visionary dreamers. Others are practical and down-to-earth doers.

Some are tenderhearted and sensitive to the feelings of others. Others put personal feelings aside and try to be fair.

Some want close emotional attachments and feel abandoned by emotional distance. Others feel suffocated by such closeness and require emotional distance for survival.

Each person is unique, of course, but there are some broad categories of personality characteristics.

The shy ones: Shy people are often respectful. They sometimes find it difficult to initiate. They are apologetic and self-effacing. At their worst they say:

"I have nothing to offer."

"Others have better ideas than I do." "They won't listen to me."
At their best they say:

"I will not intrude."

"I respect your opinions."

"I'm a good listener."

"I will encourage you."

The independent ones: These are the people who make a move toward others, but when they feel uncomfortable with what feels like too much emotional closeness, they protect themselves by backing away. At their worst they say:

"Don't fence me in."

"I'll do it my way."

"I'm self-sufficient."

At their best they say:

"I can get things done."

"I offer structure and stability."

"If it's broken, I'll fix it."

The warm ones: These people "come on strong." They are warm and caring. They may be unaware that their affection is sometimes seen as an invasion of personal space. At their worst they say:

"I'll tell you more about myself than you want to know."

"Let me hug you."

"Let's have an instant in-depth relationship."

At their best they say:

"I care about you."

"I will not wound you."

"I will listen with a sympathetic ear."

The assertive ones: Others who come across too strongly are less warm and more aggressive. They are confident of their abilities. They have a high need to be right. These are the movers and the shakers. Although they get things done, they are sometimes seen as overwhelming, abrasive, or dogmatic. At their worst they say:

"I tell it like it is."

"If you won't do it, get out of the way and let someone else do it."

"I'm right."

At their best they say:

"I know how to accomplish difficult tasks."

"The impossible takes a little longer."

"The sky's the limit."

Differences in personal style have much to do with how people function within their relationships.

Which one of the above describes you best?

1. shy one
2. independent one
3. warm one
4. assertive one

To which people do you relate best?
1. shy ones
2. independent ones
3. warm ones
4. assertive ones
With which do you have the most difficulty?
1. shy ones
2. independent ones
3. warm ones
4. assertive ones

If two shy ones are in a relationship, they may both have difficulty initiating exchange. The relationship can be conflict free; however, there may not be much energy. It may be characterized by hesitancy.

If two independent ones find themselves in a relationship, there may be structure and stability, but there may also be emotional distance. The relationship may be based on a shared task or on skill-learning.

If two warm ones get together, they will sit and commune heart-to-heart. They may forget all practical considerations, and they may be too caught up in enjoying each others' company to care. They will laugh and hug and talk and have a wonderful time.

If two assertive ones have a relationship there will be much "playing devil's advocate." These two will enjoy debate for debate's sake. There may be a high level of conflict, competition, and aggression.

What words would characterize the relationship of a warm one and an assertive one?
1. _____
2. _____
3. _____
Describe a relationship between a shy one and a warm one.
1. _____
2. _____
3. _____
If an assertive one and an independent one had to work together on a project, what do you think would result?
1. _____
2. _____
3. _____
What kind of team player would each personality be?
_____
_____

Who would be more likely to assume a leadership role?
1. shy one
2. independent one
3. warm one
4. assertive one
Who would have no difficulty cooperating?
1. shy one
2. independent one
3. warm one
4. assertive one
Who would get the work done?
1. shy one
2. independent one
3. warm one
4. assertive one
Who would be more likely to smooth conflicts?
1. shy one
2. independent one
3. warm one
4. assertive one

As you picture people with differing personal styles in relationships, it enhances your ability to observe and analyze human nature.

Fill in the blanks.
1. I would like others to think of me as _____.
2. I would like for others to help me by _____.

How to relate well to others

Recognize your own value. We are instructed by the Apostle Paul not to think of ourselves "more highly than [we] ought to think" (Rom. 12:3). Most women do not have this problem. Many women struggle against feelings of worthlessness. They have difficulty listing their positive attributes. Women typically assume blame that is not theirs. Many women apologize for fear they may have offended. It is as if they believe they do not have the right to breathe air and occupy space. In order to relate in a healthy way to another person, we need to have a sense of our own worth.

Recognize the value and worth of others. Assume a cordial and respectful stance with others. Everyone has something to teach us. An attitude of receptivity and openness to different personal styles and different views will increase our understanding and will broaden our experience. Jesus met people where He found them without respect to gender, race, social class, or religion. He met them without judgement and in a spirit of love.

Have a desire to relate well to others. There are people who prefer not to relate to anyone. Some people have withdrawn because of early wounding. Some people are angry at the world and have withdrawn. Some simply choose to be alone. Relationship implies interaction. It is risky. If we choose to relate to others, we open ourselves to pain. If, however, we isolate ourselves from others, we miss the joys life has to offer. Most of us see a need and make an effort to get along with other people. The socialization of a child is both process and task. Socialization begins early in life and continues until late into adulthood. Our lives are enriched and enhanced by the positive relationships we form. Relationship requires a conscious choice.

Develop social skills. Learn to listen with interest and without interrupting. Avoid the temptation to dominate the conversation. Read and learn so that you will have something to contribute to the relationship. Learn to use and appreciate gentle humor in your interactions. Know when humor is appropriate. Develop a consciousness about your facial expressions and body language as you interface with others. Your words may say, "I'm listening," but if you do not maintain eye contact or you turn away while the other person is speaking, your body sends the opposite message.

Ask for what you need. Often we tend to think other people can read our minds, or we believe, if they really cared about us, they would know automatically what we need or want. No one knows what another person wants or needs at any given time. State your needs and desires clearly and politely. This takes the guesswork out of relationships. Women often feel they have no right to ask for what they need. Women of a certain age were socialized to give and not receive. Our mothers and Sunday School teachers taught us through Scripture verses that our primary concern should be for others. In the process, we began to deny our legitimate needs. In a functioning relationship, we need to be able to express our desires and needs without being labeled, by ourselves or by others, as selfish or greedy.

Be willing to cooperate. Be a part of the team. Don't worry about who gets the credit. Taking a cooperative attitude encourages healthy relating. Ask a friend or co-worker, "How can I help you?" You will find that others appreciate your offer. Such an offer is a source of encouragement and shows your caring spirit.

Learn to sincerely affirm. Everyone likes and needs affirmation. We tend to give affirmation the way we would like to receive affirmation from others. Some people want a hug. If you are a toucher and a hugger, you probably will want others to touch and hug you. Some people prefer verbal praise and are accomplished at giving verbal praise to others. Consider the needs and tastes of others as you seek to affirm.

Lead in your areas of strength and allow others to lead in theirs. Give yourself permission to express your opinions on subjects about which you know you have some expertise. Do so kindly and without dogmatism. You may be able to teach someone something useful. Listen to the opinions of others. They may differ from yours. You can respect their right to believe or react in a manner different from yours. After an encounter, ask yourself, "Did I grow from this experience? Did I learn anything?" If you can answer in the affirmative, the experience can be counted as useful. Be willing to teach others. Let others teach you.

Learn to set limits. As much as you might believe otherwise, you cannot be all things to all people. It is necessary to draw boundaries around our lives and relationships in order to function well. Limits must be drawn around the issues of time, energy, and affection. A healthy relationship does not demand of us more than we can give. We will be careful not to ask of others more than they can give.

Time limits: There may be those who will consistently telephone you at three in the morning with a fresh crisis. Obviously, this is a violation of your personhood. Let it be understood that unless someone has a true medical crisis or the house is on fire, it can wait until morning.

When I was a young mother caring for a baby and a two-year-old, a woman from our church called daily and talked nonstop for an hour. No amount of telling her politely that it was inconvenient for me to talk dissuaded her from the onslaught. I simply did not know how to handle that situation. Some women want to please others and have a difficult time refusing even the most outrageous request. We may find ourselves scheduling every waking minute according to someone else's agenda, leaving no time for ourselves.

Energy limits: There are those who will require all of your energy and will use you to meet their emotional needs. You need to decide how much you can reasonably do. We are commanded to bear one another's burdens. You will find that some people don't bear any part of their own and are happy to unload on you.

Affection limits: There will be people who want more from you than you are able or willing to give. In relationships, feelings sometimes go awry. If you feel uncomfortable about the level of affection, or the manner in which someone expresses affection toward you, you need to be able to say, "I am uncomfortable. Perhaps we need to talk about this."

To know yourself, you need to look inward. To relate to others, you need to look straight across. Some people with hands on hips look down at others making demands and issuing orders. Others, with eyelids aflutter look up in a helpless manner. In order to relate well as adults, we need to look straight across at each other in openness and mutuality.

CHAPTER 3

Look back

If you have ever been on a cruise (or seen one depicted on television), one of the things you notice is that passengers are pampered to the point of absurdity. All the mundane details of life, like turning down your own bed or foraging for food, are suddenly and miraculously taken care of by someone else. You would certainly not carry your own luggage!

In case it has escaped your attention, life is not like that. As we come into adulthood, we carry our baggage with us. It has been called our bag of sorrows. There is room enough inside it, however, for more than our sorrows. All of life's experiences, all of our reactions, and attitudes are a part of what we carry. Sometimes the burden feels too heavy. Some days it is simply inconvenient and very awkward. What baggage do we carry? Everyone has at least four pieces.

The **steamer trunk** looks just like the one Missionary Lottie Moon took to China in the 1880s. It is roomy with a curved lid. It is the kind of trunk that ladies packed with finery when they took a riverboat cruise before the Civil War. It was replaced in history with the more mundane military footlocker so prized by college students. Your steamer trunk is uniquely your own. It may be loaded down and too heavy to carry. You may never have opened it to examine what's inside. On the other hand, you may have long ago dusted off the contents, decided what you would do with the items you found, and relegated the trunk to the attic.

Inside your trunk, you carry two very important items: (1) the family rules (written or unwritten) with which you grew up, and, (2) your early childhood memories.

Think of the rules your family lived by when you were a child. They may be something as simple as "children are to be seen and not heard," or "finish your homework before you watch television." Rules are simply "the way we do things."

Write two rules from your childhood family.

1. _____

2. _____

Sometimes rules have to do with money. You may recall something like this: In my family we never had enough money. Dad earned the family income and he controlled it. We never knew if he would arrive with his paycheck intact. Often he spent it at the bar before he got home. My mother had to scrimp and save in order to make ends meet.

Or, you might remember something quite different: My father was the last of the big spenders. It gave him a real boost to be able to pick up the check and pay the bill for a dinner party. It may have meant the family would not have grocery money that week, but he never seemed to think of that. My mother was tight with money. She believed that eventually all banks fail. Money should be put in a fruit jar and buried under the apple tree in the backyard so that when the next catastrophic depression comes, she would be ready.

Other rules might have to do with church attendance. The rule might simply have been: We go to church. That might mean that we went to church every time the church doors were open. It certainly meant no one slept in on Sunday morning. It might be a rule which applied only to the women and children in the family.

Your family rules shaped and influenced you. You may have grown to adulthood believing that the family rules you grew up with are right. You may not feel comfortable with any deviation from those rules.

The old legend about the grandmother who always cut the end off of the ham before she put it in the pan is instructive. Her daughter grew up watching the procedure so that, when she baked a ham, she also cut the end off. The granddaughter, seeing her grandmother and mother cutting the end off the ham, also cut the end off the hams she baked. One day she asked her mother, "Why do we always cut the end off the ham before baking it?" Mother didn't know, so she asked her mother. The grandmother answered, "I don't know why you do it. I do it because my pan is too small."

When we do things for no reason, or because we've always done it that way, there may be a family rule involved. Family rules probably made sense at one time. Some family rules no longer serve their original purpose. We keep doing things over and over because they are familiar to us, even though they are not particularly pleasant or useful.

You may have gone the other direction and vowed, "I'll never treat my children like my father treated me." You may accomplish this, but you are still very much influenced by early family rules. Your need to defy them still gives them power over you.

Your steamer trunk also contains your memories from your early life. They are an important part of the baggage we carry into adulthood.

Close your eyes and think of yourself before the age of seven. Allow the memories to rise. Picture yourself as that small child. Think of a specific event as opposed to an ongoing situation. Remember colors, clothing, voices, facial expressions, location. Feel the emotions that you felt as that small child. Open your eyes.

Write the memory that came to your mind. _____

_____

How old were you at the time of your memory? _____

Where did the event take place? _____

Who was there? _____

What happened? _____

_____

What emotions did remembering bring to your mind? _____

_____

Some people do not remember anything before the age of seven. Sometimes memories are too painful and they are blocked. Blocking memories does not happen on a conscious level. We forget for two reasons: the memories are so traumatic that we cannot allow ourselves to remember for fear of reexperiencing the pain, or the event was so trivial that it made no impression.

All of our experiences are stored in our brains. Some people remember happy events. If you are one of these, you may have written something like, "I remember the day I won the spelling bee in the second grade," or "I remember the Christmas morning when I was three and I found a big red tricycle under the tree." Other people remember traumatic events. "I remember the night my father came home drunk and beat my mother."

Much has been written and discussed about the wounded inner child. No one gets through childhood without some wounding. There are no perfect parents because our parents' parents were also wounded as children and so were their parents before them. If we need an explanation of the biblical phrase "and their children and their children's children even unto the seventh generation," this may be it.

We remember selectively. Why, out of the millions of events in your childhood, would you remember the ones you do?

If you remember mostly warm and happy events, you may have armed yourself with these good memories and you face the world expecting the best. Your trust level is, very likely, high and your relationships are mostly nurturing.

If you were the favored child in your family of origin where other children were not so favored, you may feel guilty for having escaped mistreatment while others suffered. You may have, in adulthood, put on the mask of perfection. You may have a high need to please. You may believe that if everybody likes you, or if you can just ingratiate yourself with others enough, they cannot wound you. You may be propelled by the fear that you might not please everyone.

If you remember only trauma from your early life, you may face the world expecting to be wounded. The world does not disappoint you. Your trust level is probably low and you shield yourself from pain by using any number of defenses. You may cover your pain with bravado or an excessive show of anger. You may assume an I-don't-care attitude. You very likely care very much. You may find yourself in painful relationships—relationships which do not measure up to your need for nurture. In fact, your relationship tends to bring you more pain than joy. It is not that you like being wounded over and over again. It is that it feels very familiar to you—just like home.

If you find yourself often depressed to the point you cannot function, you need to talk to a caring counselor.

A second piece of baggage you carry into adulthood is the **duffle bag**. In it you carry all the dirty laundry of a lifetime. We are all sinners who have come short of God's glory, but if the gospel has any message at all, it is that we do not have to carry our past sins and failures around with us. "Surely He has borne our griefs and carried our sorrows" (Isa. 53:4*a*). "And His stripes we are healed" (v. 5*b*). He carried griefs, sorrows, sins, guilt, shame, failures, faults. Why then, do we not allow Him to do what He promised to do. There is something about us that either does not believe that God really will forgive us. ("How could He forgive me. I am the most horrible person in the world. You don't understand the terrible things I've done. I don't deserve to be forgiven.") Or, we want to earn forgiveness ("If anyone is going to heaven it's Mary Tinsley. Look at all the nice things she does for other people. She will get past the pearly gates for sure. I'm not sure about me, but she has certainly earned her ticket.")

The person who believes Mary Tinsley is going to heaven because of all the nice things she does, needs to check out the doctrine of salvation.

The person who says, "I don't deserve to be forgiven," is right on target. God doesn't forgive us because we deserve it. God forgives us because God is Love and wants to be in a relationship with us. Although we say we believe it is not through our own efforts that we are put into right relationships with God. We sing "Jesus paid it all," but we act as if we must drag the duffle bag of dirty laundry around after us like an anchor weighing us down.

Imagine yourself carrying a heavy canvas bag on your back. Your body is bent. You have a hard time catching your breath. You are very tired of the burden. Picture Jesus carrying the cross. Walk up to Him. Put the bag on His back. Tell Jesus you do not want to carry the burden any longer. Leave it with Him. As you leave your load with Him, imagine that your body is no longer bent. The burden has been lifted off your back. You may have done this over and over during your lifetime. This time, picture yourself walking away from the bag. Do not look back. It is no longer yours to carry. Your legs no longer ache. You walk with new energy. Your breathing comes easily. There has been a release. Come to Jesus for daily cleansing. Do not let the dirty laundry pile up. The great promise of God is that there is grace greater than our sin.

A third piece of baggage we carry is the **backpack**. This is not the kind of backpack that hikers carry with all they will need on a hike. This backpack is filled with anger, animosity, rage, bitterness, and resentment—precisely the things we do not need. It is the kind of baggage that we stuff full to the point of explosion. When someone wrongs us, we add to the contents of our backpack.

Women have the reputation, perhaps undeserved, for never forgetting the wrongs done to them. It is true, however, that some women can, in an argument with a male, say something like: "I'll never forget it. It was July 23, 1973. I was wearing my blue sundress and we were getting ready to go to a family picnic. You said. . . and I said. . . and you answered. . . I'll never forget it as long as I live." This may be the same woman who says to a sibling, "Mother always loved you best."

Why do old resentments simmer? How can we finally be free of the burden of old pain? What is anger? What is it not? How can we handle the painful emotions? Anger is not a primary emotion. It covers pain and it covers fear. Anger is fuel. It is not a sin even though some may have been taught that it is.

Generally, parents prefer that children not throw tantrums. Such behavior is exhausting and inconvenient for everyone. Many parents teach children that anger is ugly, or worse, that the child is ugly when she is angry. Many of us grew up afraid of adult rage. Now that we are adults, loud voices and angry facial expressions still trigger fear in us.

The Bible does not teach that anger is sinful. "Be angry, and do not sin" (Eph. 4:26), is an indication that anger is a human emotion which we will feel. We are warned not to sin because of it. There are three unhealthy ways people handle anger.

1. They dump it. Anger can become a sin when we explode and hurt someone else. Some people are perpetually irritated. They complain and demand their way through life. When their anger level rises to the danger point, they dump rage on anyone in their path, most often, not the one who caused the anger in the first place. If they are driving a car at the time, they are a menace. If they can get their hands on a gun or knife while in this state, they can plead insanity in a court of law after they have committed murder. Anger can be pathological.

2. They deny it. If we feel that anger is a sin, we can smile and deny it to the point that we literally do not feel it. People in denial about their anger create a fantasy world where all is manageable. We do not feel anger because we do not allow ourselves to be out of control. Anger does not simply disappear, however. It will show up somewhere, sometimes as physical symptoms such as headaches, ulcers, colitis, respiratory problems, and muscle spasms.

3. They turn it inward. Anger turned inward becomes depression. Little girls who were reared to be nice may grow up into depressed women. We often have a heavy emotional investment in believing ourselves to be sweet, loving, kind, giving people. In order to maintain that image, we go to great lengths to deny our anger. We need to give ourselves permission to express anger in ways other than exploding or becoming depressed. Holding onto old resentments is self-destructive. We need to learn to let go.

What can we do with the backpack? Lay it down. Surely there is a better way to live our lives than nursing all the old wounds and inequities. One pastor suggested we develop "holy numbness." We need to ask ourselves just how much emotional energy we want to spend on old grievances. It takes energy to continually deal with all the old wrongs and the resulting anger. Anger can serve as fuel. It can be channeled in healthy directions.

The teakettle

Put a sign on your bedroom door: DO NOT DISTURB or VENTING IN PROGRESS. You may need to take the phone off the hook and enlist someone to take care of the children to ensure your privacy.

1. Sit on the side of your bed. Breathe deeply. Close your eyes and allow emotions to rise. Anger, sorrow, sadness, grief, pain—allow whatever is in the backpack to come to the surface.

2. Identify the emotions. As elementary as it may sound, say to yourself, "This is what pain feels like," or "I'm feeling anger."

3. Give yourself permission to feel whatever emotion presents itself. Your feelings belong to you. No one can say to you, "You shouldn't feel that way." You do feel that way and it is permissible.

4. Begin at the top of your head and think down to the bottom of your feet. Monitor your body. Ask yourself, Is my scalp tight? Are my temples throbbing? Does my face feel tight? Is my jaw clamped shut? Is my throat constricted? Are the muscles in my neck and shoulders tight? Do I feel pain in my neck? Are the muscles in my back in spasm? Is my chest tight? Is my heartbeat or respiration rapid? Is my stomach knotted? Is my intestinal tract in turmoil? Do I have lower back pain? Do my legs ache? Are my feet tired?

As you do the body checklist, you will discover where in your body you feel the emotion that you have identified.

5. Vent. Limit your venting to ten minutes. If you have never vented some childhood pain or rage, you will be overwhelmed by it if you try to vent it all at one time. If you are feeling hurt, you may need to cry. If you are feeling anger, you might beat the mattress with your fists or put your head in a pillow and scream. You may find that you feel somewhat foolish. Vent anyway.

6. Descend. When venting is over, lie down and breathe deeply. Take in air through your nose very slowly until you cannot take in anymore. Gulp the last bit of air through your mouth and hold it to a slow count of five. Breathe out as slowly as possible through your mouth.

7. Release. Pray. You may pray something like this: Dear God, I know you made me and you know me to the center of my being. You made me with the capacity to feel all kinds of emotions. I thank you for that capacity, even when the emotions don't feel good to me. I know that even negative emotions are a sign of life. I ask you now to take the energy I spend on my anger and pain and fear and to re-channel it into something healthy and productive that will bring honor to you and peace to me. I give it to you right now. Amen.

The last piece of baggage we carry with us is our **flight bag**. As the name implies, it is portable; it goes with us. It is full of our hopes, dreams, expectations, our fantasy of what life will be or should be. Many folks go through life chasing an impossible vision.

The myths we hold dear go something like this: "I would be happy if I had more money." "I would be happy if I could get my mother (father) to love me." "I would be happy if I found the right person to marry." "Someone else will bring me happiness." "I deserve to be happy." "Bad things will not happen to me because I am a Christian."

With this kind of expectation, life invariably disappoints and wounds. Bad things are going to happen; it is a part of the human condition. Some days will be happy, and some days you wonder why you were ever born. Chasing happiness is a sure way not to find it. Happiness is a by-product of good relationships and productive accomplishments.

We tend to think that if we have Christ in our hearts and are trusting Him, we will have happiness. Jesus never promised that. In fact, He warned, "I did not come to bring peace but a sword" (Matt. 10:34). Over the centuries, Christians have suffered for and because of their faith. Even Christian faith doesn't make all the pain go away.

Scale your flight bag down to a manageable size. It does not mean that you cut yourself off from hopes and dreams, but that you take a realistic view of life and adjust to what you can reasonably expect. Paul said, "I have learned in whatever state I am, to be content" (Phil. 4:11).

Happiness may come to you in contentment with life. Some people go through life asking, "Is this it? Is this all there is?" They are extremely disappointed. The other extreme is the person who gives up, sighs, and accepts whatever happens as "my lot in life," "my cross to bear." Can we not strike some middle ground between a headlong pursuit of an unrealistic fantasy and giving up and eating worms? Health lies in knowing who (and Whose) you are, productive work and positive relationships. Along this path, you may be surprised by happiness.

Baggage carrying is a universal phenomenon. Some baggage is heavy; some needs to be thrown overboard. Some of it is useful, and some of it we carry out of habit. Your baggage is unique, yet everyone else in the world can identify with you in the experience. We do not escape the pain of the human condition.

Years ago, in reaction to Sigmund Freud's ideas, psychologists said that past experiences of our lives were not relevant. People should accept responsibility, forget what is past, and get on with life. That is true if it means we should not allow the past to paralyze us. It is also true that we are unable to get on with our lives as long as we have not examined our baggage. The process is somewhat frightening, but having examined our past, we have a better understanding of who we are. We find courage to face life with God's help. We understand that we share some common joys and sorrows with the human family. It is one way we join the human race. In order to look forward—to get on with our lives—we must look back.

CHAPTER 4

Look out

Relationships do not always develop in healthy and mutually satisfying directions. When pain, fear, or distrust dominate, the relationship needs to be evaluated and corrective measures implemented.

Think of a relationship which has endured over the years—a friendship, a marriage, or a relationship with a blood relative.

Is this relationship nourishing?

1. Does the other person express appreciation for your contribution to the relationship?
2. Does that person express verbal affection to you?
3. Do you sense that the other person enjoys being with you?
4. Do you feel at ease when you are with the other person?
5. Do you believe the other person considers you a positive influence in her/his life?
6. Do you believe there is a realistic balance between the efforts you put into the relationship and the rewards you experience?

Is this relationship toxic?

1. Does the other person often criticize you?
2. Do you find that the other person talks more about your mistakes than your accomplishments?
3. Do you feel that affirmation is withheld from you by the other person?
4. Does the other person frequently lose her/his temper with you?
5. Does the other person yell at you?
6. Does the other person put you down in the presence of others?

Do you recognize these people? Everyone knows an **Annabelle**. She is angry, abrupt, abrasive, and opinionated. She offends, but the one thing you can say for her is that she is consistent. She does not pick and choose the people she accuses, suspects, wounds, intimidates, and offends. She does it to everyone in her path.

Beverly reacts by being compliant. Beverly finds herself looking for reasons which explain Annabelle's behavior. Beverly believes that Annabelle must have had a particularly difficult childhood; she can't help the way she treats people. Annabelle may not feel well today or someone was rude to her. Annabelle has it harder than most people. If it snows, the snow is always deeper at Annabelle's house. Beverly walks on eggs around Annabelle. She does not like walking on eggs, but she feels it is her Christian duty to forgive 70 times 7 (though, to be sure, Annabelle has never asked forgiveness; she feels justified in what others recognize as her appalling behavior). Beverly loses sleep over the relationship and often has stomach problems, but she believes the best way to deal with Annabelle is to let her have her way and just suffer through. She knows being a martyr is not the healthiest or most attractive thing to do, but she is afraid to act any other way. Annabelle seems so strong.

What's wrong with this picture?

1. There is no excuse for Annabelle's behavior.
2. Annabelle does not assume responsibility for her own behavior.
3. Beverly is too heavily invested in the relationship. She has given Annabelle too much power over her life.
4. Allowing Annabelle to have her own way is counterproductive.
5. Fear-based relationships are unhealthy.
6. Annabelle is not strong. She is aggressive and intimidating, but that is often a sign of weakness, not strength. Her need to intimidate is a clue that under all the bluster and bravado exists a very insecure, wounded, and fearful person. Her attitude seems to be, "I'll hurt you before you have a chance to hurt me." Her abrasiveness is a defense against pain and one that keeps others at a distance.

Carol also has been offended by Annabelle. Her method of dealing with the situation is to retaliate. Carol is not going to take anything from someone like Annabelle. If Annabelle has a need to control, she is going to get a taste of her own medicine. Carol feels that Annabelle will try to take over the whole world. She is probably the most obnoxious and controlling person ever to set foot on God's green earth. She is a bulldozer—loud, lumbering, and dangerous enough to destroy anything that gets in her way. If that's the way Annabelle's going to play, Carol will meet her toe-to-toe. On her better days, Carol knows that her own behavior toward Annabelle is not particularly Christian.

What's wrong with this picture?

1. Carol is reacting. She is caught up in her own anger. She thinks she is in control, but Annabelle is still calling the shots.

2. Carol has entered into a competition to see who can be more controlling and abrasive.
3. Carol is aiding and abetting Annabelle in a destructive pattern.

Diane also has been offended and wounded by Annabelle. She has simply decided to cut Annabelle out of her life. She will, as needed from time to time, be in the same room with Annabelle, but emotionally, Diane has opted out. She has withdrawn from the field of battle. Her mother always told her, "There are some people you are better off ignoring." If ever there was someone who deserved to be cut out, it's Annabelle. Yet, Diane struggles with the concept; it makes her uneasy. She wonders how a Christian should handle this kind of relationship.

What's wrong with this picture?
1. Christians do not have a right to ignore other people.
2. Diane is engaging in either/or thinking—she must either carry Annabelle around as an emotional burden, or withdraw completely.
3. Diane can generate other options. These scenarios represent three different ways of dealing with the same situation: placate, retaliate, or distance. None is healthy or effective. Each sets up more of the same. The behavior that needs to be changed is, instead, intensified. The more Annabelle intimidates, the more Beverly placates. The more Beverly placates, the more Annabelle intimidates. The more Annabelle controls, the more Carol retaliates. The more Carol retaliates, the more Annabelle feels she must control. The more Annabelle behaves in an appalling manner, the more Diane distances from her. The more Diane distances, the more Annabelle feels she must behave badly to get Diane's attention.

How do we deal with the Annabelles in our lives?

It is not OK for Annabelle to act the way she does. In spite of her childhood wounding, in spite of the deep snow at her house, it is not permissible to treat people the way she treats them. The early wounding may be a reason for her behavior, but it is not an excuse. We are accountable and responsible for our own behavior—not that of others, but our own. We cannot help the way we feel. We can begin to change the way we think. We can always control the way we behave.

Beverly, the martyr, is helping neither Annabelle nor herself by tolerating Annabelle's behavior. It is not only permissible, but desirable, to set boundaries and limits. The rationale behind boundary setting goes like this: This is where I draw the line. Behind the line is where I live. It represents my private space. My personhood is within this space. If I allow you to continue to treat me in a disrespectful manner, I feel that I am allowing you to violate my innermost self. I do not wish to wound you or offend you, but I cannot allow you to continue to speak to me or act toward me in this way.

Retaliation is not the way to deal with people like Annabelle. The attitude of *I'll get you for that,* is not one that fosters health and peace of mind. Retaliation tends to escalate the conflict, and no one wins. Control and countercontrol gets into the unproductive game of one-upsmanship. When one person thinks, *I've won,* the other combatant comes up with something even more wounding. The relationship becomes a battleground and there are no survivors.

Distancing is a way of protecting one's self from pain. We distance by being too busy or too tired or too sick. Diane made a conscious decision in regard to Annabelle. *I am not open to you.* She is saying, *I do not care about you. I feel nothing for you. If you were sick I would not try to help you. If you need someone in a crisis, don't call me. I do not care.*

Apathy is the ultimate insult. As Christians, we must care. Does Jesus love Annabelle? Did He die for her? Are we required to tolerate her behavior? Are we required to ask for added grace to love her? A wise person once said that Christian love is not some emotional burden you carry around. It is, instead, the sincere desire that another person will enjoy God's very best. Can we wish God's best for Annabelle?

How do you recognize inappropriate behavior?

If you have doubts about what is appropriate and what is not, check the following questions.

1. Is it immoral, unethical, or illegal? If you are behaving in any way that breaks the law or violates God's laws, the behavior is inappropriate. Dishonesty, lying, cheating, stealing, adultery, murder—all the "big" sins are out of bounds. Most of us breathe a sigh of relief and say, "That lets me off the hook."

2. Is it manipulative? Is my behavior an attempt to try to coerce someone else to change their behavior to suit my agenda? Manipulation is a form of emotional blackmail. The underlying message is, "If you do what I want, I will reward you," or "If you do not do what I want, I will punish you." The reward may be nothing more than my approval. Punishment could be as simple as my disapproval or my withdrawal from you.

3. Is it self-serving? People whose goal in life is their own self-aggrandizement act in inappropriate ways. They set out to have their own way at the expense of others. Most often, if behavior is not for the common good, we may judge it to be inappropriate.

4. Is it malicious? Evil exists in people's hearts and in their behavior. If the intention is to wound, humiliate, frighten, intimidate, or shame another person, the behavior is malicious. Purposely holding another person up to ridicule, pointing out defects or deformities, name-calling, embarrassing someone publicly, putting someone down—all are examples of malice. If you have been the recipient of any of these, you have no difficulty recognizing the behavior. It takes the form of verbal, emotional, or psychological abuse.

5. Is it out-of-control? Has the anger turned to rage? Has the indignation become hysterical? Has the telling become overdramatic and histrionic? Does the behavior call attention to itself and make others uncomfortable? It is inappropriate to ordinary social exchange.

6. Is it a misuse of power? If a large person takes advantage of a small person, it is a misuse of power. The small person may be a child whose life is in the hands of a parent or teacher. The small person may be an abused spouse. The smaller person may be an employee whose livelihood depends on doing what the boss demands. The smaller person may be the more reticent or less confident of two friends. The large person may be physically larger, richer, stronger, or higher up on the corporate ladder. Anytime a larger or more powerful person violates the integrity and rights of another and uses size, status, or threats to do so, the behavior is inappropriate.

There is a difference between power-grabbing and empowering. Sandra Hamilton, a pastoral counselor in Richmond, Virginia, explains that some people think of power as a pie. They own the whole pie. They invest in keeping it all. If another person has power, it is construed as a theft of a slice of the pie. Think of power as a candle instead of a pie. If you have a lighted candle and someone else has an unlit one, they can light their candle from yours. Has anyone stolen anything from you? Is there now more light? Is there more warmth? Was this a theft? Is this a metaphor for mutuality and healthy relationship? Empowering another is an act of healthy relating.

7. Is there turf protecting? Think of someone you know who feels he must protect what he considers his turf. In one tradition-bound group, the women were planning their annual Christmas party. A newcomer suggested a wonderful punch recipe and volunteered to make it. A hush fell. Every woman present turned a shocked face upon her. Someone said in incredulous and reverential tones, "Katie makes the punch." Obviously, the punch was Katie's turf.

All animals and some people are territorial—not likely to share with others. We can choose to give up our territory and open ourselves to the ideas and suggestions of others.

8. Is it one up/one down? There are people who cannot feel good about themselves—they don't feel up unless someone else is down. Any verbal put-down is designed to put the speaker up. Appropriate behavior dictates equality in value of two people in an interchange, and mutual respectful treatment.

There are three directions we look as we relate to others: up, down, and straight across. Looking up often means we are fawning, trying to impress, or manipulate. When we look down, we have our hands on our hips, figuratively if not literally. We are going to tell it like it is. This brings almost immediate satisfaction because of a rush of power, but we literally put someone else down in order to feel good for a moment.

The appropriate way to talk to another person is straight across—no hidden agenda, no manipulation, no intimidation. "This is what I think," or "What do you need?"

CHAPTER 5

Look up

When you choose to be in a relationship with another person, you are either open and vulnerable, or suspicious and defensive. Whether you are in a relationship which involves deep, personal feelings, or in a relationship on a less intimate level, you make yourself vulnerable to another person. In fact, one definition of love is simply making yourself vulnerable to someone else. When you love, you give another person power over you, and you trust that person not to take pleasure in wounding you.

All relationships involve risk. Relationship involves our willingness to trust in and be vulnerable to another person. Friendship implies trust. You can assume that a friend wishes good things and not evil. A friend will not knowingly inflict pain on you. A friend will not betray you. Even in a superficial working relationship, one trusts the other person to work toward common goals for the general good. This requires, if not love or friendship, at least good will and honest intentions.

My relationship vision

1. Relationship is _____
2. Honesty is _____
3. Affirmation is _____
4. Availability is _____
5. Caring is _____
6. Communication is _____
7. Commitment is _____
8. Understanding is _____
9. Intimacy is _____
10. A friend is _____

Women in the Bible—lessons in teamwork

When Paul wrote to his young friend, Timothy, on the subject of women, his letter was highly instructive. In chapter 2 of 1 Timothy, Paul advises that women should dress modestly, be of quiet demeanor, live a godly life, be learners, be forbidden to teach men, and be silent.

In chapter 5 he gives more advice: treat older women as you would treat your mother. Treat younger women as you would treat your sister. Widows are problematic. Don't let any widows under the age of 60 be a member of your church, and then only if they formerly have brought up children, lodged strangers, washed the feet of the saints, relieved the afflicted, and diligently followed every good work. The (presumably younger) widow who is desolate and alone should trust God, pray night and day, show piety at home, and bring honor to her parents. Don't let young widows be members of the church under any condition. They tend to be wanton. They should remarry so they will be busy running their own households. They will, then, not turn into gossips and busy-bodies, saying things they shouldn't say.

One wonders what Paul would say about women in the church today! If we want to learn about women in the Bible and their relationships, we must look at the women themselves. Their lives were not easy, but their experiences in many ways parallel the lives of women in all times and places. We see them relating to each other in familiar ways.

The women whose names grace the pages of Scripture never heard the word *teamwork*, yet they practiced the concept. Where women are mentioned in the Bible, they are often portrayed as engaging in a cooperative effort to accomplish some task.

Luke 8:1-3 mentions the 12 disciples that were with Jesus and certain women are named—Mary Magdalene, Joanna the wife of Herod's steward, and Susanna. There are many others not named, but the task of these women was to "minister to Him of their sustenance." These women who followed Jesus "throughout every city and village" worked together to form a group that provided financial support for our Lord's ministry. Very likely, they also took care of some logistical details of daily life. Does that sound familiar?

Use a sanctified imagination. Put yourself in the group of women who followed Jesus. What sort of relationships do you believe developed within that group? What do you imagine the women talked about among themselves? What sort of bonding took place? Was there laughter as they prepared meals for the 13 itinerant preachers? Can you imagine suggesting someone put more water in the soup? Were there intimate talks about family problems and personal concerns? Were there disagreements? Did they cry and comfort each other? The common cause of Christ must have bonded them together then, just as it bonds us now.

In other Scriptures we find women at work together propelled by a common purpose. In the 11th chapter of John, Jesus visits in the home of his friends, Mary, Martha, and Lazarus. We see Martha complaining that Mary sat down to listen. We do not know what happened before Jesus' arrival. Perhaps Mary had done her share of cleaning and carrying water. It was the women who did the necessary preparation for the arrival of this loved guest. It is not surprising that Lazarus is not mentioned during the disagreement over kitchen duty. No one expected him to peel potatoes.

Are you a Mary or a Martha?

Mary was
  a listener and a learner
  more contemplative
  spiritually attuned
  quiet
  a searcher for truth
Martha was
  a doer
  practical minded
  concerned about people's needs
  hospitable
  house proud
Perhaps in different circumstances you are both. Mary and Martha each had something to offer. Can you see positive qualities in both?

There is not a more tender story in all of Scripture than that of Ruth. Ruth and Naomi, mother-in-law and daughter-in-law, bonded together by a common sorrow, loved each other and decided to stay together. Naomi advised the younger woman in how to attract Boaz as a husband, thus providing the women with security in a society where women had no protection without a male. So worthy was Ruth, and so kindly did God look upon her, that she is one of the four women named as an ancestress of Jesus in the genealogy at the beginning of Matthew's gospel.

Write the name of one of your female relatives (either by blood or by marriage). _____

What is the relationship? _____

What qualities does she possess that make her attractive to you? _____

_____

What experiences have you shared which bonded you together? _____

_____

_____

Elizabeth, six months pregnant with John the Baptist, visited Mary (Luke 1) who had just learned that she was to bear Messiah. The two women, who were obviously very close to each other, sat, talked, and marvelled at the wonder of the promise of these two little boys who were yet to be born. They surely provided emotional support for one another. Their task of rearing two such special children must have loomed large. They encouraged and affirmed each other.

If you have borne a child, do you remember being pregnant? _____

_____

Do you remember a friend who was also expecting a baby during your pregnancy? _____

Recall what it was like to talk together. What emotions did you feel?

_____

If you have not had a child, do you remember working on a project in which you were heavily invested emotionally? _____

What comes to mind? _____

_____

Did you have someone during that time who was your sounding board?

_____

Recall what it was like to talk together. What emotions did you feel?

_____

Paul commends his son in the faith, Timothy (2 Tim. 1:5). He mentions Timothy's grandmother, Lois, and his mother, Eunice, as ones in whom the faith first dwelled. Imagine the mother's cooperation with her grown daughter as they worked together to teach the young Timothy.

In the Lois-Eunice-Timothy relationship we see several family connections: mother-daughter, mother-son, grandmother-grandson.

List some words and phrases that characterize your relationship with your mother:

_____

_____

_____

Do you remember your grandmother? What do you remember of your relationship to her when you were a child? List some of those memories.

_____

_____

How much influence do you believe your mother and grandmother(s) had/have on you? _____

_____ _____

_____

_____

The resurrection passages in Matthew, Mark, Luke, and John tell of the women's appearance at the tomb. Imagine these women, sorrowing and stricken by shock, but nevertheless doing what they believed was the last thing they could do for their Lord. The anointing of the dead body involved wrapping it in strips of linen after placing spices and ointments for embalming. The spices used for this purpose, myrrh and aloes, were expensive. Again, we see women spending not only their money, but themselves, bonded together by a common belief, a common experience, and a common task. List three women with whom you work in your church.

1. _____
2. _____
3. _____

What are the tasks you set out to accomplish? How would you characterize the relationship you have with these women? Are there any positive changes you would like to see in any one of these relationships? If so, how do you see these changes occurring?

There are many other women in Scripture who were wise or kind: Abigail (1 Sam. 25) who prepared food for King David's men and averted bloodshed; Dorcas (Acts 9:36) who was extolled for her kindness in sewing garments for widows and orphans; Lydia (Acts 16:14*ff*) who prayed at the riverside and then hospitably opened her home for a house church; Deborah (Judges 4), the prophetess who judged Israel; Esther, who saved her people; Mary (John 12:3), who anointed Jesus' feet with costly ointment. Priscilla (Acts 18), who taught doctrine along with her husband. With which of these women do you identify?

There are unnamed women—the carriers of water, the grinders of grain, the preparers of food, the sewers of garments, the bearers and caretakers of children. Who packed the lad's lunch that fed thousands? Who made and placed the pillow in the stern of the ship on which Jesus, exhausted, rested his head during the storm? Who cooked the dinner at Simon's house?

Do you ever feel unrecognized for all you do? Look around you. We are everywhere. There are other unnamed women who need an encouraging word from you. When we adopt a team spirit, a spirit of cooperation, our work is made lighter and we receive the bonus of relationship.

Coping skills

There are many coping skills we can adopt which will ensure teamwork in our relationships. They include learning how to solve problems, knowing how to deal with difficult people, learning to speak up, learning to let go, learning to reframe, and choosing better ways to relate.

How to solve a problem

1. Agree on the definition of the problem. Has the meaning of the problem for each person been made clear?
2. Agree on a time to negotiate.
3. Agree that negotiations will take place between two calm adults who can talk without allowing the talk to escalate into an argument.
4. Agree on the deadline for solving the problem.
5. Agree on whether or not it is possible to expand the time available before a final decision must be made.
6. Agree that some things probably won't change. Define these.
7. Agree that solving the problem is more important that holding on to a particular solution.
8. Agree that both are open to new and familiar solutions.
9. Agree that there are resources to help. Define these.
10. Agree to appropriate available resources.

If two people can agree to the ten steps above, solving the problem is possible. Both persons will need to let go of the idea of winning so that creative solutions to the problem can be generated.

11. Solve the problem. There may be some issues on which two people will need to agree to disagree and give each other permission to think, or act in ways other than what they both believe is right.
12. The last and most neglected step to problem solving is to restore the relationship. This can be done by generating some high energy activity done together which brings laughter.

Years ago, a wise mother would give each of her two squabbling children soft, clean rags and some window cleaning solution. She put the children on opposite sides of the glass with instructions to make it shine. The two grumpy faces invariably turned to smiles and then laughter. When two adults find themselves irritated or angry and argumentative, the situation can be defused with laughter. Playing kazoos, singing a song, jumping up and down, making faces at each other—these activities and many others can help to restore the good will and good feelings between two former combatants.

Dealing with difficult people
1. Anticipate. You have dealt with this person before or you have dealt with a person like this one. What can you expect? Is this person out of control with anger? Will this person blame you? Will this person give you the silent treatment? Will there be pouting or other forms of manipulation? Anticipate.
2. Hesitate. When in doubt, don't. Hot words may come to your lips, or you may feel intimidated and overwhelmed by fear. You may feel a need to ask questions. Resist these impulses. This is like counting to ten before you speak when you are angry. Pause and gather your wits about you. Unless the person is confronting you with a gun, pausing will give you a sense of calm.
3. Evaluate. What is the situation? What does this person want and need? Why is this person acting this way? Is there a solution to the problem? What are the options? Can you respond with some sympathy and calm? Do you need to remove yourself until the situation calms?
4. Communicate forthrightly and in a kind manner. "I have thought it through , and while your point of view is valid, I believe. . . I feel. . . I would like. . . I have decided. . . . "

Learning to speak up
   Think of someone who has wounded you in the past. It may be a parent, a sibling, a spouse, a friend, a co-worker or a boss. In the following exercise, underline or add words which apply.
• When you do not listen to me I feel dismissed, angry, retaliatory, unimportant, _____.
• When you withdraw from me I feel abandoned, rejected, distanced, guilty _____.
• When you use sarcasm (literally "a hole in the flesh") I feel diminished, wounded, put down, angry, _____.
• When you speak harshly in anger I feel afraid, defensive, anxious, devastated, enraged, betrayed, _____.
• When you give me the silent treatment, I feel anxious, left out, guilty, powerless, _____.
• When you blame me or accuse me, I feel defensive, angry, fearful, _____.
• When you do not accept responsibility for your own behavior and try to exonerate yourself, I feel angry, unfairly blamed, accused, _____.

Learning to let go

Remember an embarrassing incident in your life. Recall the circumstances of the event and answer these questions:

When did the event take place? _____

Where did it take place? _____

Who witnessed it? _____

What were the circumstances of the event? _____

What words did I speak? _____

What did others say? _____

What emotions did I feel at the time? _____

What emotions do I feel now recalling the incident? _____

Imagine that in your left hand you hold the emotions you felt at the time of the event. Imagine that in your right hand you hold the ones you feel now. Clench your fists. Hold onto the emotions with all your strength. Choose to open your fists. Let your hands relax. Imagine the negative, painful emotions flowing away from you as water would flow between your fingers. Let them go.

Clean up

Today I cleaned out drawers and closets.
I threw away an accumulation of bits and pieces,
Odds and ends—
Well, to be truthful,—junk—
Faithfully carted from place to place for 20 years.
I tossed a crumbling corsage from the senior prom
Along with brittle, yellow newspaper clippings
from the dim and distant past.
I tossed stacks of term papers and efforts at handwork,
homework assignments
And old letters.
I threw away photographs—
Of people no one could identify,
Of college friends I haven't seen for 25 years
And very likely never will again,
Blurry ones,
Faded ones,
Six copies of the ones we had seven copies of,
Aunts and uncles and cousins five times removed—
Old clothes and paperback books—
A mountain of trash!
It was cathartic, this clearing out,
And along with the trash I tossed some old dependencies.
Resentments, too, went the way of the trash barrel.
I got rid of a few worn-out ideas, some old regrets,
Old dreams long outgrown,
And two or three outmoded behavior patterns.
I felt as if I'd leaned on the door of my prison cell
Only to have it swing open because it was never locked.
I felt a lightness,
A freedom,
A release of spirit.
It was a good day—
A most satisfactory day.

Learning to reframe

Reframing means looking at a situation from a different angle, or seeing something from a different point of view. Your cousin is selfish. She is angry all the time. She complains to everyone about her miserable life. She has a tendency to hurt your feelings with her harsh words. You have always feared her and felt that she was a very strong, demanding, and controlling person. You have felt that she dislikes you and takes delight in hurting you. Close your eyes and imagine your cousin as a small child. What has wounded her? Was someone cruel to her? Was she the scapegoat of the family? See her as weak and powerless. See her as frightened. She is afraid she will never receive love. Feel tenderness toward her. Take her into your arms and give her comfort. See yourself affirming her for her talents and her abilities. See yourself opening your heart to her in love. You have just reframed. It is as if you have been looking through one narrow lens and have seen from one perspective. Suddenly, you put a telephoto lens on your camera, and you see that there is more than meets the eye. You can reframe your attitudes, your way of doing things, and your way of relating to others. Reframing offers us choices.

Defining a creative relationship

1. I will approach the other person with trust. I will tell myself that the other person has a right to feel the way she/he feels.

2. I will listen to the other person. I will not only listen with my ears, but with my eyes, and with my emotions. I will try to read the underlying meaning in what the other person is saying, and not limit my listening to the words that are being spoken.

3. I will learn to clarify. I will ask questions and makes statements that reframe what the other person is trying to convey. ("I think I understand. Do you mean. . . ?) or ("You seem to feel. . . . Is that correct?)

4. I will not try to defend my point of view, point out the truth, or explain the way it really is.

5. I will draw boundaries (behind which I live and a violation of which would cause me pain) by giving information ("I feel that. . . " "I don't like it when. . . " "I feel misunderstood when. . . "). I will not try to change the other person.

6. I will defend my territory by quietly stating what I will do in various circumstances. This will be offered without anger or accusations, not as a threat, but calmly to give information to the other person.

7. I will state my desire to explore options with the other person in order that creative solutions can be found and implemented.

Relationship configurations

A hierarchy is just what the name implies: two or more people are in a relationship with a clearly delineated pattern of power. Someone is in charge. The person in charge has power over the people who are not in charge. In any hierarchy, there is an imbalance of power. This happens anywhere there is a corporate body, although it can happen in marriages and friendships as well. Hierarchies occur in church life, in educational systems, in the military, in government, and family life.

The person in charge is the one with power. Power is obtained by election (as in government), by ascription (agreement that a certain sort of person will just naturally be in charge), or by working one's way up the ladder to the top. The people not in charge are responsible directly or indirectly to the person in charge.

In our society the people in charge have status. The things that confer status are money, physical size, education, and expertise. In Christian churches we speak of humility, servanthood, and equality, but we are impressed by power.

The hierarchy looks like this:

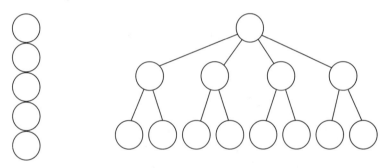

In a 50/50 deal there is an attitude of quid pro quo, that is something for something. There is the agreement that we will be in a relationship, but I will only put in as much as I get out of it, and you will only put in as much as you get out of it. If and when either of us feels we are putting more in than we are getting out, we can withdraw from the relationship. This arrangement sounds equitable. There is nothing wrong with it except that it doesn't work. Two people cannot be in a relationship that is entirely equal and fair at all times. In a relationship, expect to give more than you get.

I listened to a group of women plan what they would do for each other should any of them ever have to go to the hospital. They made detailed plans about the amount of money to be spent and what kind of flowers to order. The discussion came about because one woman had received cut flowers and another a potted plant during their respective hospital stays. Such energy spent over such nonsense! It takes the joy out of giving and turns a gift into a right.

The 50/50 deal looks like this:

A better way looks like this:

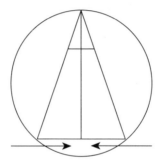

The circle represents God's love, protection, and grace around us, the everlasting arms beneath us, and God's guidance over us. The triangle is a symbol of God's being a part of human relationships. The verticle line of the cross represents our relationship to God. The horizontal cross beam symbolizes our relationship to others. The bottom line of the triangle represents the level ground at the foot of the cross where we find room enough for everyone in God's inclusiveness.

Relational theology
Our God is the One who comes to us, the great initiator of relationship. Genesis 3:8-9 says, "And they [Adam and Eve] heard the sound of the Lord God walking in the garden in the cool of the day, and Adam and his wife hid themselves from the presence of the Lord God among the trees of the garden. Then the Lord God called to Adam and said to him, 'Where are you?'" All of Scripture is the story of God's overtures to and relationship with people. It is the record of the God who Self dis-

closes. What we know of God is what God has chosen to reveal to us.

In the Old Testament, we know about God through creation, mighty acts, personal contact with selected individuals, and through covenant promises, prophets, priests, and kings. God made the covenant with Abraham in Genesis 12:2-3: "I will make you a great nation; I will bless you and make your name great; and you shall be a blessing. . . . and in you all the families of the earth will be blessed." It was God who broke into human history speaking words of promise and command to Moses and the prophets. The New Testament is the story of God made flesh—God with us. In the fullness of time, God's last and best Word appeared on the human landscape—Emmanuel. "'Behold, a virgin shall be with child, and bear a Son, and they shall call His name Immanuel,' which is translated, God with us" (Matt. 1:23).

There is nothing more significant in all of history than the cross and resurrection event. It was God's gift to us of life, worth, blessing, and hope. God invites us to be half of a relationship.

Revelation 3:20 says, "Behold, I stand at the door and knock. If anyone hears My voice and opens the door, I will come in to him and dine with him, and he with Me."

We are invited to be in relationship with God just as others have been invited since the dawn of creation. We can have daily access to and fellowship with God. Through Christ we are restored into right relationship and are returned to the original blessing of creation when God said, "That's very good."

The nature of the relationship between God and humankind is everlasting and is based on God's faithfulness and God's promise. Romans 8:38-39 says, "For I am persuaded that neither death, nor life, nor angels nor principalities nor powers, nor things present nor things to come, nor height nor depth, nor any other created thing, shall be able to separate us from the love of God which is in Christ Jesus our Lord."

Our relationship with God is secure in Christ. Our God is faithful to the promises that we will not be forsaken. Here, finally, is the answer to our fears. We are terrorized by thoughts of abandonment. If you were ever separated from your parents as a child, you may recall the panic of being lost, separated from the adult who was responsible for your safety.

Old fears come washing over us. We read the newspapers. We live in a violent and unsafe world. We seek safety. We are afraid of being alone. We seek comfort. We have suffered grievous loss. We have suffered betrayal from someone we thought was our friend. Loved ones die and leave us heartsore and stricken by shock and grief. Circumstances conspire to frighten us with the specter of poverty, illness, old age, and death. We cast about to find security. Where is there permanency in a world gone crazy? Only in Christ.

This faithful God who comes to us and brings to us our rooting and our grounding, shows us, in Christ, how to live.

Seeing ourselves through God's eyes

"God saw everything that He had made, and indeed, it was very good"(Gen. 1:31).

This was the original blessing God gave to humankind. God created us good and declared us good. This first blessing has sometimes been overshadowed by our need for redemption, but God did not create anything that was not good. Because God made us and redeemed us, we are no longer estranged.

Why should God want to have a relationship with us? Have you ever made a quilt, or baked a pie, or designed or made a dress? Do you remember the sense of accomplishment and pride you took in that simple act? Imagine how much more God takes pride in the created order. Imagine the pleasure God takes in having relationship with the crown of creation. We can begin to see ourselves, then, as God sees us: worthy and valuable.

A young North American visited a Brazilian family. He wanted to take them out to a restaurant in order to thank them for their kind and loving hospitality. The elderly mother, who had spent years preparing meals for her family, had never been inside a restaurant. She watched the others prepare to go out. When the young man arrived, he asked if everyone was ready to go. She shyly looked up and asked, "You mean me, too?" God says to us with open arms and a loving smile, "Of course, I mean you, too." The message of the gospel is one of inclusion.

Relational theology dictates how we relate to others

At the point of our relationships one with another, our faith becomes practical. If faith has worth, it is lived out in our behavior.

It is easy to think holy thoughts on Sunday morning on pew number three. It is much more difficult to put those thoughts into loving actions when we are dealing with each other Monday through Saturday.

Scripture teaches us how to treat each other. Consider this dialogue between scriptural admonition and one struggling woman.

"Bear one another's burdens, and so fulfill the law of Christ" (Gal. 6:2).

OK. I'll check that one off my list. I can do that. In fact, I'm good at that. I am a caring listener and I'll help anyone who is in trouble. That's easy. It comes naturally to me.

62

"Let all bitterness, wrath, anger, clamor, and evil speaking be put away from you, with all malice. And be kind to one another, tenderhearted, forgiving one another, just as God in Christ also forgave you" (Eph. 4:31-32).

Now, that is a little more difficult. I don't see myself as a hateful person, but there have been times when people were mean to me. It takes a little more doing to forgive. I know God forgave me, but after all God is God and I'm just a struggling little person. It's a lot harder for me.

"He who covers a transgression seeks love, But he who repeats a matter separates the best of friends" (Prov. 17:9).

If I forgive, I know there are benefits all the way around. The relationship will be restored and that's good. I don't have to carry the pain of it around with me anymore. That might be nice.

"Beloved, let us love one another, for love is of God; and everyone who loves is born of God and knows God" (1 John 4:7).

There are people who are easy to love. There are people who require an extra measure of effort and grace. Why can't everyone be as nice as I am?

No doubt, other Scriptures will come to mind that have to do with relationship and you have your own response to them.

If we need a picture of how to relate to each other, we have it in the example of the three persons of the Trinity: God the Father, the Son, and the Holy Spirit. Observe what is present within that relationship: The Father sent the Son to be the Saviour of the world. The Son was sent by the Father. The Holy Spirit, said Augustine, is the link of love between the Father and the Son. What characterizes this relationship? What words describe it? Unity, oneness, cooperation, mutuality, love, commitment, sacrifice, willingness, sharing, selflessness, giving, gifting, trust. By contrast, what is absent from the relationship? We find no power grabbing, greediness, self-aggrandizement, self-pity, malice, or competition.

We can take the triune God as our definition of productive relationship. We can know how to relate to God and to each other. The thrust of Scripture deals with the ethical implications of our faith. It dictates the way we are to behave within our relationships. How can we say we love God if we don't love our neighbor, or our husbands, or our friends, or the women with whom we serve in our church? One of the first Bible verses we teach children is "Be kind one to another." Because God is love, we live in love and behave in loving ways.

CONCLUSION

We were juniors and seniors in high school. We belonged to the church youth group. This was where we received Bible teaching and lessons in morality, where we made professions of faith and tried to find God's will for our lives. In that church that we found our spiritual sustenance but also our social life, our emotional support, and our affirmation. We were, as a group, inseparable. We sang in the youth choir and passed notes down the row when we were supposed to be listening to a sermon. We went on youth retreats and participated in youth revivals together. We exchanged sweaters and boyfriends with equal frequency. Our parents more or less trusted us when we were all together, and they endured, with as much grace as they could muster, the loss of sleep our giggles and shrieks caused at our slumber parties. With solemnity we looked at each other and vowed to be forever friends!

The years crept—no, flew—by. Geography and life choices separated us, but memories and shared experiences bound our hearts over the years and miles. Not long ago we celebrated a 40th reunion. We decorated the house for Christmas, although it was late summer. There beside the glowing tree, we opened our heart gifts. It was a time of remembering and thanksgiving. We recalled events of long ago. We remembered a loved pastor and those leaders in our youth group who had given us so much of their love and time and energy. Some memories brought laughter; some brought tears.

Such an experience is rare in these times. Our society is mobile and moves at an astonishing rate. Divorce has fragmented the lives of almost everyone and remarriage often means blending families. Work fills our lives with too many long hours. No one can remain aloof to issues—alcohol and drug abuse, family violence, war, poverty, and injustice. When we look around us, we feel overwhelmed.

It is not possible to go back 40 years to a more innocent time. Women today are making different kinds of choices. They struggle with questions of identity—whether or not to marry, whether or not to bear children, supporting themselves and often their dependents, blending career with family responsibilities, being safe in an unsafe world.

Women are accomplishing things today that would make our grandmothers either gasp in astonishment or stand up and cheer. And yet, not everything has changed. Wherever there are women, there will be intimate talk. There will be nurturing, and caring, and laughter. There will be interest in color, and texture, and beauty. Women will ask each other for advice, for a shoulder to cry on, for a helping hand with the children or with plans for the open house. There will be women who prepare the food and teach the young—basic, elemental life-giving and life-enhancing activities. Women will be there, just as they were at the foot of the cross and at the tomb on resurrection Sunday, ready to weep, but eager to believe and rejoice. They will do these things in groups or two by two. It is how they do it best—within relationships.

Celebration

Let us celebrate relationship:

Not surface ("My, it's cold today." "Please pass the butter.")

Not symbiotic ("Meet my needs." "I can't live without you.")

Not manipulative ("If you love me you'll. . . " "With all your talent and capability, I'm sure you'll. . . ")

Not competitive (Straight *A*'s. . . knocked the top. . . " "Why can't you be more like Martha Ann White? She. . . ")

Not condemnatory ("You're feeling sorry for yourself." "That just shows your lack of faith.")

No, not these,

But an honest opening of the self to another,

And an unconditional acceptance of that other.

Relationship! Oh, rare and precious commodity!

It cannot be forced, coaxed, or cajoled,

But freely given,

Freely accepted.

It grows in the fertile soil of listening/caring/touching.

It is reciprocal:

Seeing into another's soul

While opening my own soul's window.

Let us celebrate relationship,

you and I.

Let us fill the crystal goblet to the brim with Cana's wine.

You sip from its rim

And then let me drink, too,

In celebration and in gratitude for this good miracle.

Church Study Course

Relationship Skills is course number 03352 in the subject area: Christian Growth and Service.

Credit for the course may be obtained in two ways: (1) conference or class—read the book and participate in a 2½-hour study; (2) individual study—read the book, do the personal learning activities, and have a church leader check written work.

Request credit on Form 725 Church Study Course Enrollment/Credit Request (rev.) available from the Church Study Course Awards Office, 127 Ninth Avenue, North, Nashville, TN 37234.

Complete details about the Church Study Course system, courses available, and diplomas offered is in the Church Study Course Catalog available from the Church Study Course Awards Office.